AF477799

Ramin Haerizadeh
Rokni Haerizadeh
Hesam Rahmanian

MOUSSE PUBLISHING

This book was made possible thanks to
Gallery Isabelle van den Eynde and Alserkal Avenue

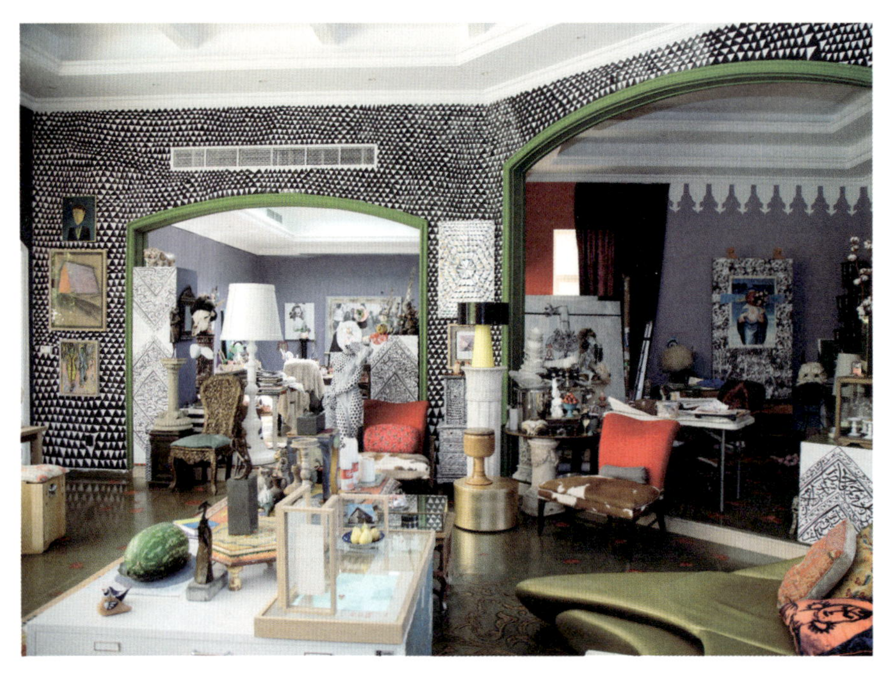

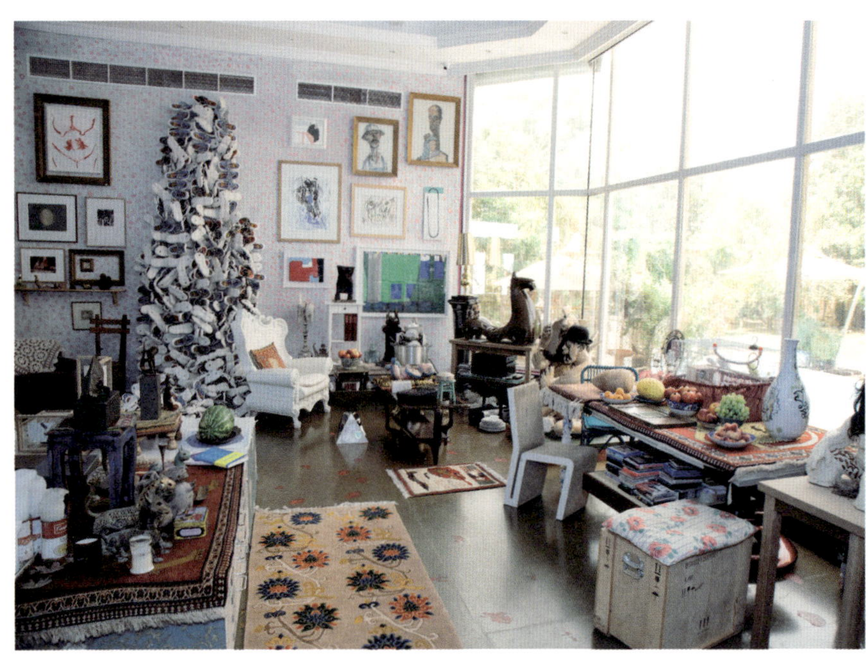

INTRODUCTION
by Daniel Baumann

This may well be a model for how to collaborate and combine; how to
build an aesthetic and undermine it; how to be politically acute and irreverent,
generous and eccentric. Eccentric not in the sense of "extravagant", but as
"away from the centre" – three Iranian artists living and working in Dubai. Yet
Dubai may be more central than Zürich or Paris, and not just geographically
but economically also.

Arriving at Al Barsha 2, Villa 100, at the house where Ramin Haerizadeh,
Rokni Haerizadeh and Hesam Rahmanian currently live, one might think,
"Wow, this is eccentric." And yet although their house is an extraordinary villa
and a studio, it is also a film set and movie theatre, a museum and research centre.
It is a test site-cum-monastery, an academy-cum-pleasure dome. The house
informs their art as it results from both collective and individual endeavour. Yet
they are not a distinct group or collective, there is no name or label for the
three artists' collaboration – one even wonders if their names might be uncanny
masks, similar to the ones they wear in their films.

The collaboration of Ramin Haerizadeh, Rokni Haerizadeh and Hesam
Rahmanian translates into multiple forms – films, installations, artworks and
exhibitions – and often evolves around other artists and friends. This includes
Iranian artist Niyaz Azadikhah and her sister, a DJ, Nesa Azadikhah, Iranian
sculptor Bita Fayyazi, polyglot writer Nazli Ghassemi, American artist Lonnie
Holley, gallery manager Minnie McIntyre, Maaziar Sadr, who works for a
telecommunications company in the Emirates, and Tamil friends Edward St
and Indrani Sirisena. Sometimes these people occupy central roles, sometimes
they are marginal, but in either case they bring with them a reality that
interrupts the trio's universe and language, and channels their attention in
unexpected territories.

Another important strategy in their practice is the inclusion of various
artistic worlds that are as respectfully acknowledged as they are shamelessly
appropriated and adapted. This ranges from artworks and objects held in their
own private collection to broader aspects of Iranian culture. Confronted with
their projects, their thinking and art-making, one can learn a great deal about
how Iranian artists have absorbed modernity – how, for instance, filmmakers,
cartoonists and artists such as Ardeshir Mohasses, Ali Hatami, Mahmoud

Khan Saba, Kamran Shirdel, or Noureddin Zarrinkelk combined Persian culture with Western influences and vernacular traditions. One realises that there is another chapter of (dissident) modernity yet to be written.

Thirdly, and quite surprisingly, there is the way in which, from their seemingly baroque setting, the three artists approach politics in their work. This is never achieved through outright illustration but via purposefully ambiguous parables that ask as many questions as they answer. Yes, the trio live in Dubai, unable to return to Iran due to the content of their work, but they never pose as "artists in exile" as the media would love to portray them. They criticise Iran's Green Revolution as much as they question normative thinking about sexuality, the roles we impose on ourselves and the art world's mechanisms – the power of curators, for instance, or the art market's obsession with branding. If there is something quixotic at play in their refusal of categorisation, it is not simply to hold a mirror up to such processes but to keep art and thinking unbound.

Al Barsha 2, Villa 100 is the core of a centrifugal world where divergent directions (and laughter) abound, and where one starts to wonder how it all holds together. Through aesthetics, I would argue, through the languages that they develop (and are still developing), and through that thing called art, which, in their case, is of stunning precision and craft backed up by broad, passionate, and generously-shared knowledge. This makes their collaboration a model for how to approach a multi-directional, if not multi-chaotic, world as well as an art institution like Kunsthalle Zürich.

As the new director of Kunsthalle Zürich, I am very grateful to begin my programme with Ramin Haerizadeh, Rokni Haerizadeh and Hesam Rahmanian and to offer, with this publication, an irreverently curated introduction to their art, their (political) thinking and, importantly, their humour.

A COLLECTIVE BODY
by Tina Kukielski

"We make a dwelling in the evening air,
In which being there together is enough."
—Wallace Stevens, excerpt from "Final Soliloquy of the Interior Paramour"

The life and work of Ramin Haerizadeh, Rokni Haerizadeh and Hesam Rahmanian represent a radical redefinition of the collective. Since 2009, the trio have transformed a nondescript villa in Dubai, United Arab Emirates, into a wondrous world for collaborative living and working: a utopia of self-sustaining creative life.

Much like the kitschy, dense, and spirited universe in which they cohabit, the imaginative realms they construct collectively as both artworks and delirious exhibitions draw on improvisational collage, assemblage and figurative painting. By casting themselves and a select group of friends as actor-protagonists in video and photo-based works, they demonstrate a buffooning and whimsical approach to exhibition-cum-theatre. Taken in combination, these strategies attest to a bewitching collective unconscious that is the crux of this joyous collaboration.

Brothers Ramin and Rokni first met Hesam in the mid-1990s, and they bonded over a shared enthusiasm for VHS tapes – containing snippets of MTV and VIVA Polska – that were illegally distributed around Tehran at that time. Their paths diverged momentarily as the three young men found their own circuitous path to art, navigating a culture bound up by the conservatism of an Islamic Republic, until they reunited in the newfound refuge of Dubai.

Though their individual artistic practices differ stylistically, consistent across the work of all three is hilarious, unyielding satire. Rahmanian studied calligraphy and fine art in Tehran and continued to pursue the latter at university in the United States. In his moody yet crisp paintings, surfaces of thick paint convey tragicomic scenes, from isolated, mundane interactions like crossing the street to more overt confrontations like a boxing match or bullfight. Rokni Haerizadeh, whose hand is more wild than the gentle and refined Rahmanian, mines the traditions of Persian literature and painting, both of which he studied in Tehran. Subverting this education in the classics, he

III

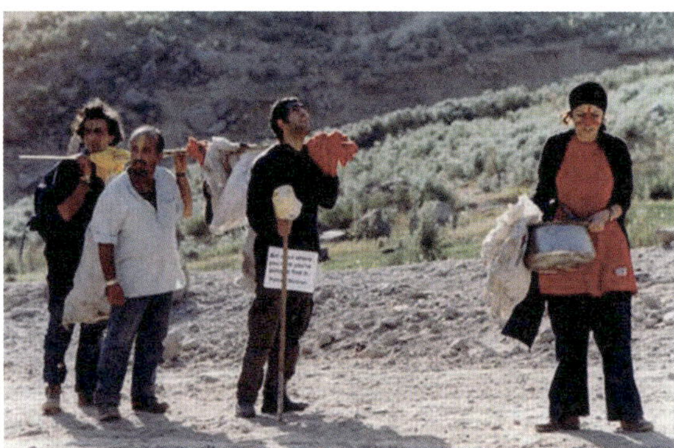

Polur, Iran, 2002

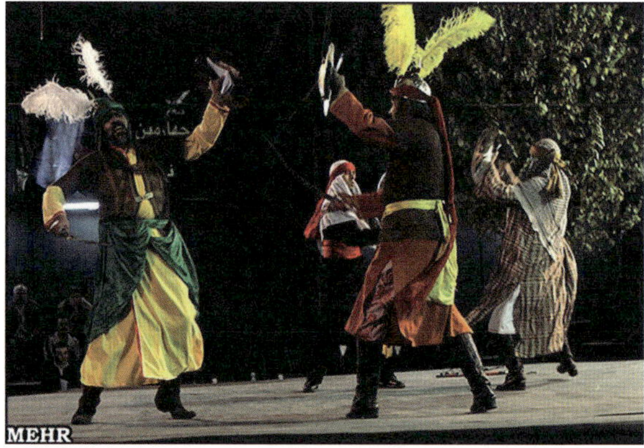

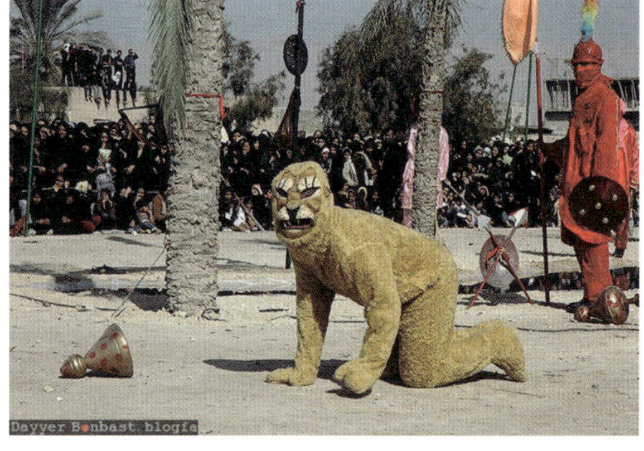

Ta'ziyeh, Iran, Mehr News Agency

IV

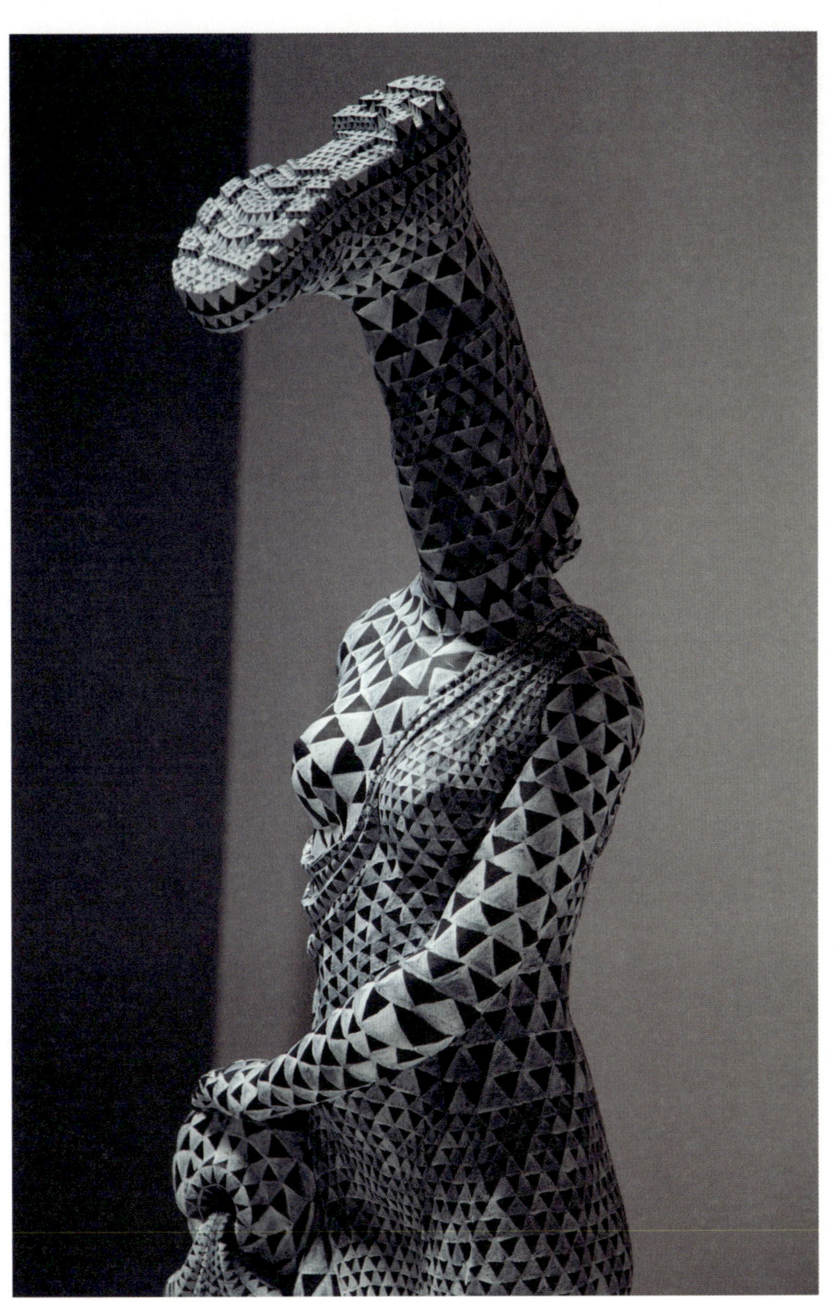

Ramin Haerizadeh, Rokni Haerizadeh, and Hesam Rahmanian, *Venus of Wellington*, 2014
Readymade fibreglass sculpture, acrylic paint, waterproof ink and rubber boot
176 x 47 x 22 cm

V

revamps scenes of newsworthy disasters, wars, or protests, like those recently
staged by the radical feminist group Femen, retelling them as twisted,
dark, and humorous allegories of human-beast metamorphosis. The work of
Ramin Haerizadeh, the eldest of the trio and the most digitally-savvy, merges
photo-based self-portraiture with appropriated materials that often erupt
from the canvas into the surrounding space. Turning collage into assemblage,
Haerizadeh thereby refigures his body-based compositions into an image-
stew of gender-bending satire.

The trio's collective vocabulary is grounded in a mutual, self-taught education in Persian poetry, British music, American art, and cinema from Japan,
Russia, France and Iran. These influences are no longer shared via contra-
band VHS but are instead sought out online, in mail-order books and through
occasional travel (though rarely does one travel without his companions). They
pool these influences, and meld them to the figurative and theatrical traditions from Iran that are ingrained in their psyches. Yet to dissect the references
in these works is to hamper an overall understanding of their transgressive
message. This intermingling of allusions, styles and aesthetic forms is better
understood as pastiche: The sediment of source material makes its particulars
subservient to the whole. The approach here is not dead, neutral "blank parody",
as Fredric Jameson once defined pastiche.[1] Rather, pastiche mobilises satire and
subversion in the interest of challenging norms about what art can be, and how
to live as artists bound between public and private, religious and secular worlds.

Up North

The seeds of the trio's collective revolution were sown as early as 2002.
Back then, it was common for Tehran's artists to gather once a year in and
around the rural mountain village of Polur, Iran, for an environmental art
festival. Participants crafted sculptures from flowers or rocks, and hung works
made from natural materials in and among the hills and trees. Occasionally,
something was set alight, but otherwise the event tended to be rather tame. For
the 2002 edition of the festival, Ramin and Rokni Haerizaedeh, along with a
small group of fellow artists and friends, had driven up from Tehran for the
festivities. Bored by the limitations of the sanctioned interventions, the group,
altogether spontaneously, began to collect the trash left behind by the other
participants: discarded flora or bamboo, and strewn plastic bags that once held
artists' projects. Eventually, this irreverent faction began to load up the flotsam

VI

from the surrounding village also, bundling their findings together on long
sticks and looking like vagabonds on their way to the next pit-stop. Soon a small
crowd assembled and the local residents began to join the makeshift procession,
helping to gather the refuse, not knowing the purpose of the absurd exercise but
improvising on it nonetheless.

The audiences amassed in Polur for the festival neglected to notice this
disruption. It served only as a minor incident, a spontaneous action without fan-
fare; a kind of *dérive* in the Situationist sense. But that day up in Polur also
had echoes of a boisterous yet serious *Ta'ziyeh*, a dramatic tradition still popular
in Iran. A form of passion play, recounting the martyrdom of Husayn (grand-
son of the prophet Mohammed), *Ta'ziyeh* makes use of various vernacular art
forms such as procession and pageantry, and is improvised on the street by
male actors. The real artistry of *Ta'ziyeh*, however, is in its bricolage costume-
making and set design. The form has been described as a disposable sacred
art because of the commonplace materials used such as found wood and bamboo
for the stage set and frame, tin foil, mica and glass for ornamentation. Costumes
are colourful and enhance the fluid dynamic between actors and audience; the
spectators are surrounded by and often drawn into the physical action of the play.
This union of piousness, participation and pageantry makes *Ta'ziyeh* a forbear
of that spontaneous performative clean-up in Polur, as well as the spirit of pastiche
and improvisation in the recent collaboration of the three artists.

Body Talk

Across the trio's diverse and copious production – whether completed collaboratively or as individual artists – the most prominent and recurring subject is
the body. Through collage, sculpture, painting and video, a myriad of bodily
representations arise: men morph into zebras, faux-antique jars become bawdy
bottom-heavy tourists, arabesques anthropomorphise into hair, eyes and mouth,
beautiful women turn selfish, violent criminals, and grandmothers transform
into garden caryatids. As such, the body is manifest at points along a broad
spectrum, from animal to human, male to female, young to old, good to evil,
thereby giving credence to theorist Judith Butler's redefinition of the body as a
"variable boundary." Here, the culturally-constructed body is made suspect
and challenged through its performance and activation as "a region of cultural
unruliness and disorder."[2] The chaos and untidiness we find in the trio's
collaborative works, therefore, equates to the obfuscation and variability of

several things at once: body image, object relation, and the performance of gender. With that comes a wellspring of implied eroticism as subtext.

Nowhere is this more evident than in the various couplings and sexual personas parodied in *Joyous Treatise* (pages 24 – 33), an ongoing series of collages that pastiche Persian illuminated manuscripts and miniature paintings. *Risala-i-Dilqusha* (*Joyous Treatise*), by the poet and satirist Ubayd-i Zakani, is a fourteenth-century book of vignettes about romantic and carnal love, each deployed as social commentary. Comparable to Giovanni Boccaccio's *The Decameron*, the manuscript is remarkable for its humour and frankness about sexual and social mores of the day. Written in both Arabic and Farsi, it was illustrated over and over again as the book circulated around the region, despite on-and-off censorship due to its salacious subject matter.[3]

Figurative art as storytelling occupies a long history in Iranian art and this provides an endless source of inspiration for the trio. In their updated version of the *Joyous Treatise*, the parts of husband, wife, lover, cheater, mistress, mother, and father are acted out by the artists and their friends. Photographed and then glued into collaged pages, surrounded by Arabic and Farsi calligraphy by Iman Raad, the figures are later altered and illuminated again with costume, colourful patterning and small glimpses of anthropomorphism. One such collage shows a scene of a husband and his pregnant wife, both equally bulbous, equally feminine, and both incidentally played by Ramin Haerizadeh (page 29). Its accompanying text refers to Zakani's original: "While Muzabbid's wife was pregnant, she looked at his face and said, 'Woe to me if what is in my belly should look like you.' 'Woe to you if it should not!' he replied." As performative satire, these works meld humour with a brew of eroticism that can only be defined as multivalent. These embellished pages are a crystallisation or mirroring of the trio's domestic life; playing dress-up and acting-out parts with each other and friends in their shared home. These already evocative stories of heterosexual or homosexual love are made even more kinky and weird via this collaborative retelling.

Fetish 1 and *Fetish 2* (pages 18 and 20) are two long scroll-like collages that erode the boundaries of the body even further. They depict a pair of animal-ballerina statues – one is upright, the other upside down, both are equally ghastly. The medusa-like head in *Fetish 1* is composed of photographs of shells and a disembodied, hairy upper torso. This figure balances atop a patterned box with its legs spread just enough to give birth to a giant fish from its bloodied centre. *Fetish 2*, dons a tutu and dancing shoes while balancing upside down on a painted sword. Again, its head is a cropped torso surrounded by creeping tendrils of finely-painted white hair. These collages arise from cut-up photographs of various body parts – some belonging to the artists, others to a cast of sitters – that have been reassembled to build a monumental androgynous figure, a paper doll, an exquisite corpse. Whether these works are seen as abject surrogates to be lauded, or composite gods to be appeased, the scale of the works alone demands attention. That they depict gender-bending, human-beast hybrids only bolsters their effect as symbols of the corporeal blurring of the trio.

Exhibition as Allusion

Take any installation by these artists and pervasive throughout is a mood that transcends the body-subject addressed above. This sentiment abounds largely due to a painted, patterned floor that unites sprawling exhibition rooms like a mirage. A cascade of black and white triangles invites the viewer to enter, but the patterns quickly become inconsistent and scatter into a sea of painted red poppies. Geometric outcroppings, evocative of arabesques, blend and morph into a screaming giant's head with a swirling shock of blue hair. Like entering *Grimm's Fairy Tales*, intimations of retreat and contemplation reverberate with moments of mystery and intrigue.

Such sensory and visual discord is a frequent tactic in these exhibitions, as is the inclusion of artworks by other artists. In an approach similar to Rosemarie Trockel in her exhibition-as-*Wunderkammer* (cabinet of curiosities), where the artist intermingles her work with that of other artists, the trio align their work through object juxtaposition by including the work of artists they admire. This has created a pantheon of artistic allusions embedded in their otherwise difficult-to-characterise approach to exhibition-making.

This self-made canon ranges from eighteenth century satirical lithographs by Thomas Rowlandson to reproductions of Francisco Goya's dark social commentaries. Oddball cartoons by musician and artist Daniel Johnston sit alongside drawings by the quick-witted Iranian satirist Ardeshir Mohasses. Figurative paintings by Nicole Eisenman, David Hockney, Tala Madani and Abel Auer also feature, as do drawings by Mona Hatoum and Louise Bourgeois. A large sculptural work built from cheap plastic sandals by Hassan Sharif, a pioneer of conceptual art in the United Arab Emirates, becomes a prop in the performative *Foolad* (pages 78 – 79), a video work filmed in the artists' Dubai home. Iranian art figures prominently as well, and modernists like Bahman Mohassess,

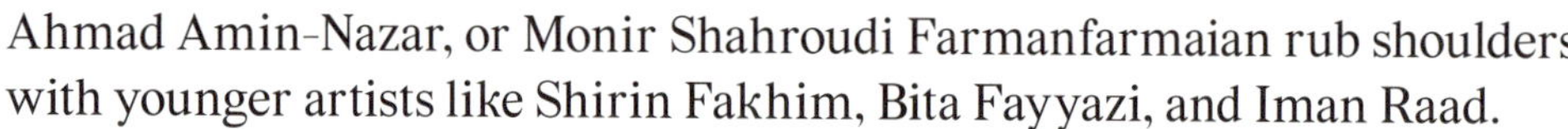

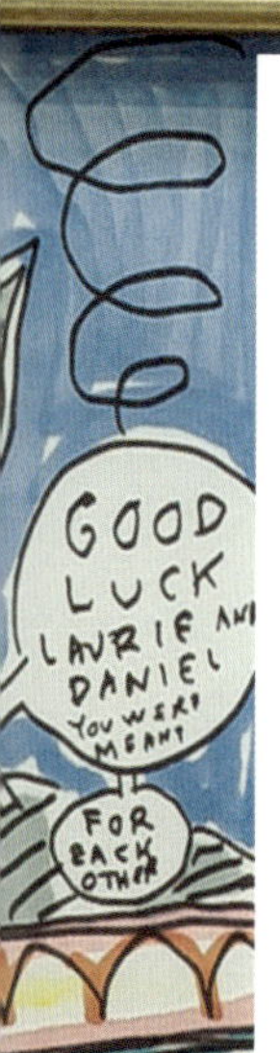

Ahmad Amin-Nazar, or Monir Shahroudi Farmanfarmaian rub shoulders with younger artists like Shirin Fakhim, Bita Fayyazi, and Iman Raad.

In the trio's first collaborative exhibition, *I Put It There You Name It* (2012), large-scale collages spread across the walls are parodies and subversions of the typical propaganda murals used to tout a political campaign, honour lost soldiers, or promote a royal family. Yet the honoured figures are not martyrs or mullahs but rather the elder female stateswomen of art and culture (pages 34 – 39): Etel Adnan, Aisha Al Marta, Laurie Anderson, Pina Bausch, Patti Smith, Elizabeth Taylor, and Vivienne Westwood among others. Even Divine and Robert Mapplethorpe make an appearance in drag not far from a winged Ayatollah Khomeini.

The use of allusion and appropriation is amplified in the trio's second collaborative exhibition, *The Exquisite Corpse Shall Drink the New Wine* (2014), whether it is works by self-taught artist and musician Lonnie Holley or those of performative-activists Guerrilla Girls. A pair of Mike Kelley's *Little Friend* plush toys greeted visitors at the entrance to *The Exquisite Corpse*; their logos read, "I watch you" a tongue-in-cheek nod to Big Brother surveillance and a reminder that, as watchers, we also are being watched. Kelly's kitschy wonderland of double-entendres and psychological inquiry is an apt connection here: Across multiple rooms, the exhibitions of Ramin Haerizadeh, Rokni Haerizadeh and Hesam Rahmanian unfold like a quasi-surrealist, quasi-domestic fantasy.

Exhibition as Theatre

These exhibitions operate like theatre in that objects are placed around the exhibition area and take on prop-like qualities as they compliment other artworks. Such *objets trouvés* range from fake-Classical statues to orange traffic cones, dolls and mannequins to oddball costume accessories of all kinds: tutus, helmets, wigs, jewellery, and striped socks. To find these readymades, the trio drive around Dubai and neighbouring Sharjah, where they collect crafts, artefacts, and cheap made-in-China collectibles.

These objects are also activated on video via improvised performances, which emerge spontaneously and are edited into coherence after the event. General yet loose rules apply to the discordancy of the videos, namely that studies on object relation are central to the action on screen. Some of these readymades embody silly or kitsch qualities, such as an inflatable lobster or rainbow-coloured pool toy. Some objects come from the domestic realm like

X

a tin of tea or bowl of fruit, while others suggest a potentially violent taboo like a knife or gun. As non-art, these objects take on a fetishistic quality as a means of transmission or translation of an unconscious system that often dictates and directs the work.

Cheap plastic masks are another recurring *objet trouvé* in these videos and serve to distance the wearer from the surrounding action. The masks feature prominently in *O, You People!* (pages 82 – 87) where the trio assume their recurring alter-egos – Rokni and Ramin as rosy-cheeked pigs and Hesam as a long-faced sheep. Made on Captiva Island, once home to Robert Rauschenberg, the video is a fetishistic encounter with the late artist's tranquil boathouse, where the trio peer into windows, or around corners, do small jittery dances, or sniff and rub their nipples on the dock. One of several videos recorded as part of a multidisciplinary residency supported by the Robert Rauschenberg Foundation, *O, You People!* is part-homage to a progenitor of pop art, part-slapstick comedy. Accompanying their curious stuttering movements on screen, is a series of voiceovers repeating a sorrowful poem by the Iranian modern poet Nima Yushij, writing about divides of class and privilege. Drawing on their own displacement as artists, further displaced by their temporary relocation to the American South on an artist residency, the trio perform a kind of ritualistic, ceremonial communion by fawning and caressing the site in adulation. As such, the intercourse between artists and the charged modernist structure becomes a sentimental yet humorous study on cultural, personal, and artistic difference.

The videos (page 72 – 87) demonstrate a diverse range of styles and cinematic strategies, indicative of the shared visual vocabulary of the collective. Notable is *We Are the Eighth of a Kind*, a visually and sonically-thrilling sound and dance tableaux improvised with fellow Rauschenberg artist-in-residence Lonnie Holley. Most videos, however, are made with friends in the artists' home in Dubai. Arranged into short vignettes, similar to the aphoristic format of the *Joyous Treatise*, these videos employ various narrative threads without pointing towards a clear story arc. Unlike *Joyous Treatise*, any outright sexual content is absent in the videos – instead of intercourse, we witness the innocent act of playing doctor, for instance. The videos tap into a Paul McCarthy-esque approach to body-based performance that is notably more chaste: scenes of dancing or fighting, public ceremonies, courting rituals, domestic scenes, and plenty of just goofing around.

The movie styles appropriated range from Bollywood to the films of Jacques Tati or Charlie Chaplin; silent films to video games or grainy cell phone footage of protests found on Youtube and social media. Each of the artists

XI

appear frequently in their own videos, alongside a rotating cast of collaborators, friends, actors and musicians. Bodies appear and disappear, they dance or make trance-like motions that border on giddiness. The body as "variable boundary" again plays out here through intentionally bad stereotypes performed for the camera: the butcher, the film star, the maid, the doctor, the drag queen — a subtle reminder that Butler's gendered body is inherently performative. That these exaggerated actions and stock characters translate across different cultures is one reason they frequently recur as motifs. As a vehicle for satire, such simple and recognisable characterisations leave the door open for interpretation by the broadest possible audience.

The spirit of spontaneity and overall design embodied in the shared enter-prise of Ramin Haerizadeh, Rokni Haerizadeh and Hesam Rahmanian takes lessons from sources far and wide, East and West, theatre and art. Their collab-oration weds these influences to an improvisational intuition that is fluent in various media and comfortable moving between private and public realms. At their most essential, the works challenge how and what can be termed art: equal parts do-it-yourself artistry, free-wheeling impersonation, action and non-action. The collective tries things the wrong way around, they make use of the useless and, in that way, cast light on subjects in the margins. This collaborative, day-to-day practice, then, is its own form of disposable sacred art, its own *Ta'ziyeh*. "Embracing what is considered marginal, wasted, wrong, messed-up, useless and the taken for granted, this becomes a stimulus for something we call an achievement," they write in a shared statement. And what an achievement it is — a union of heart, mind and soul in the interest of collective transformation.

1 Fredric Jameson, *Postmodernism, or, the Cultural Logic of Late Capitalism* (Durham: Duke UP, 1991); 19.

2 Judith Butler, *Gender Trouble: Feminism and the Subversion of Identity* (New York and London: Routledge, 1990); 177-178.

3 *Joyous Treatise* became popular in the 14th century during the Timurid Empire, a period notable in the history of Islamic art and culture due to its ruler Timur's policy of transporting and consolidating artists and craftspeople from across conquered lands to the capital in Samarkand and later Herat, resulting in great patronage and production for the arts.

XII

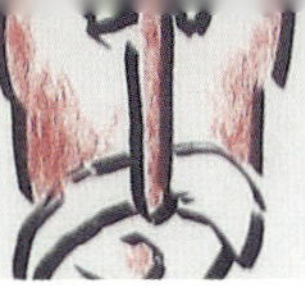

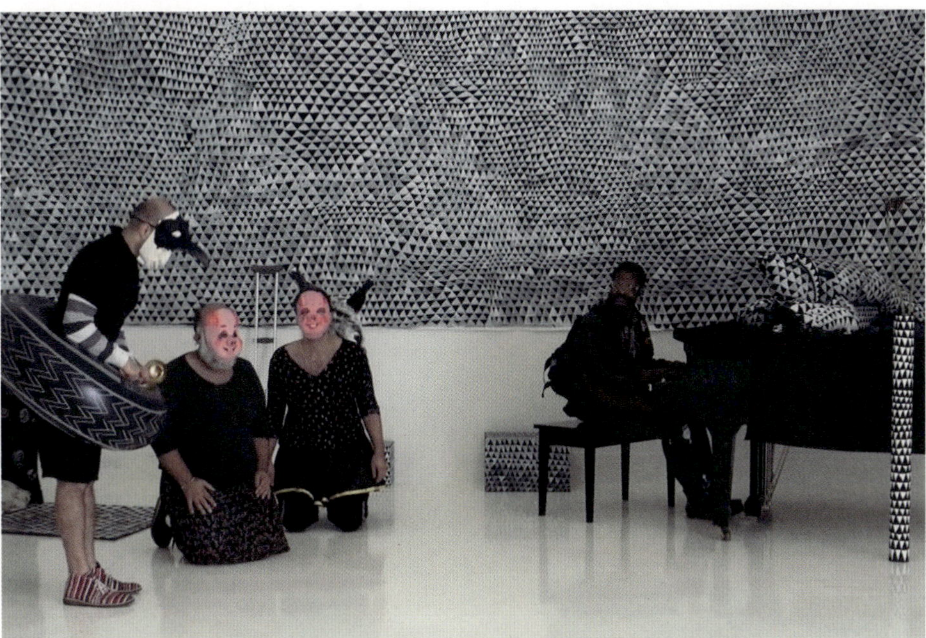

Still from *We Are The Eighth of a Kind*, 2014,
featuring Lonnie Holley

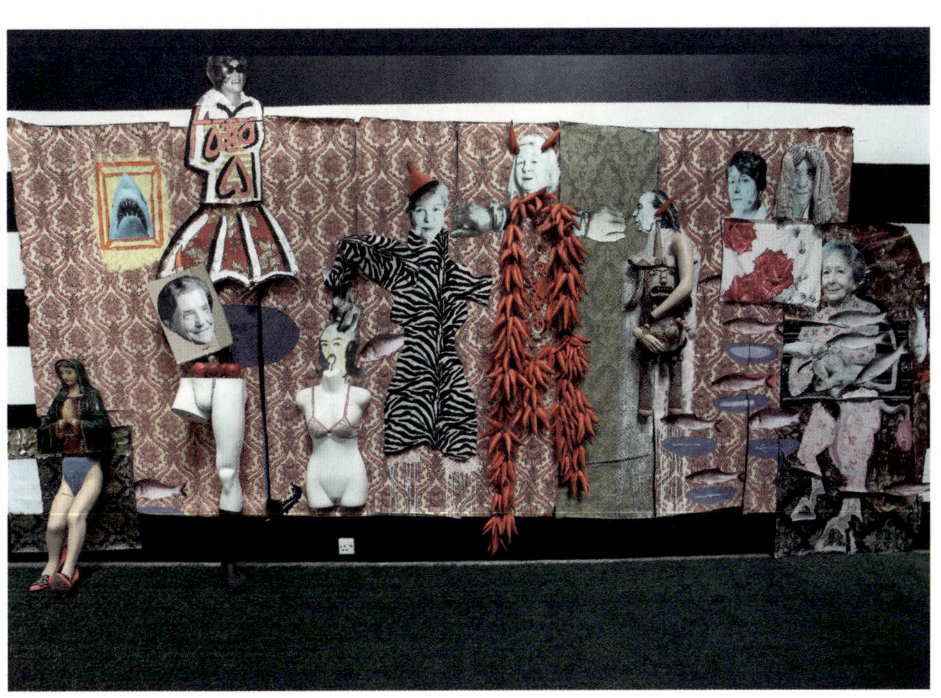

Installation view, *I Put It There You Name It*, 2012

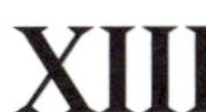

XIII

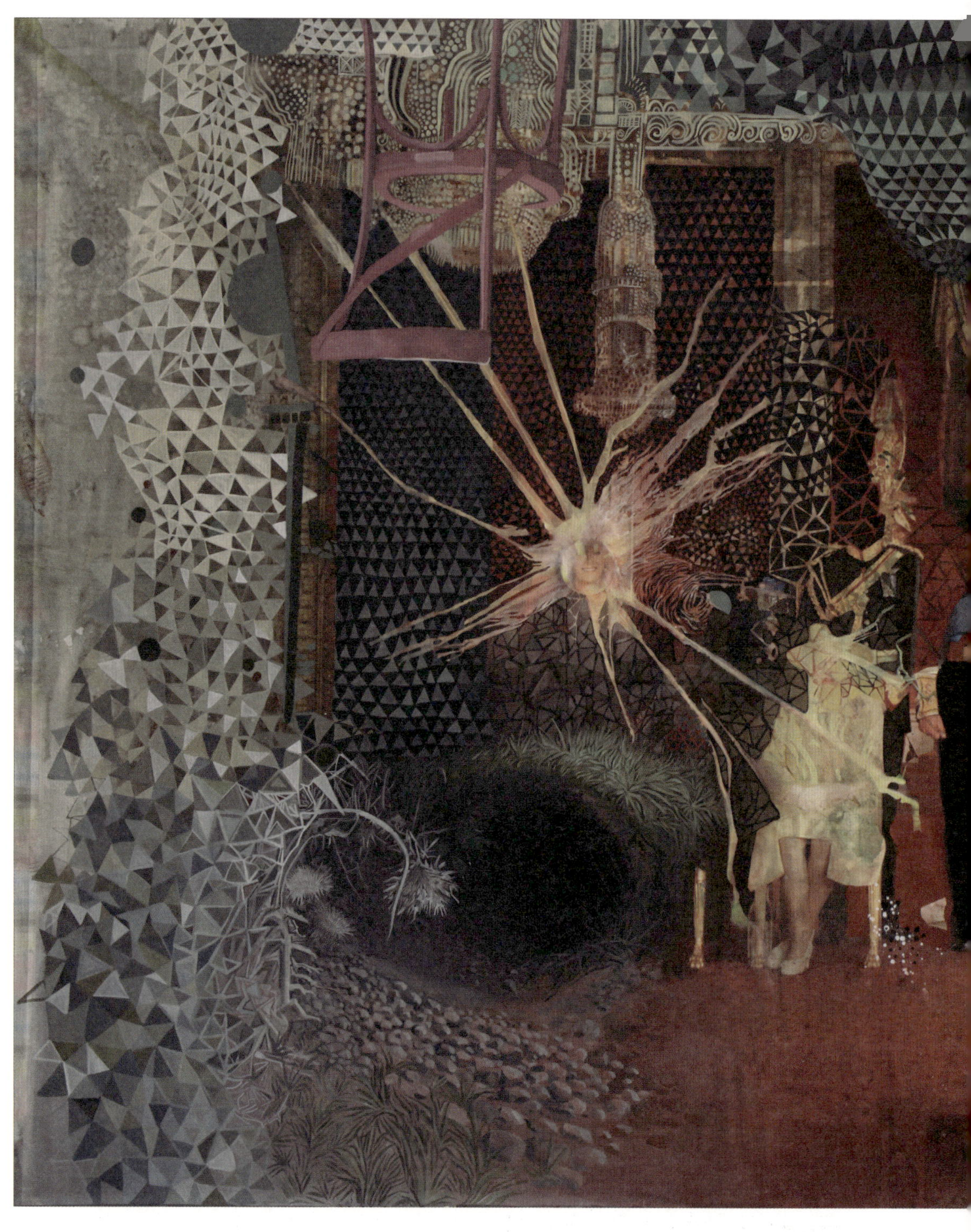

XIV

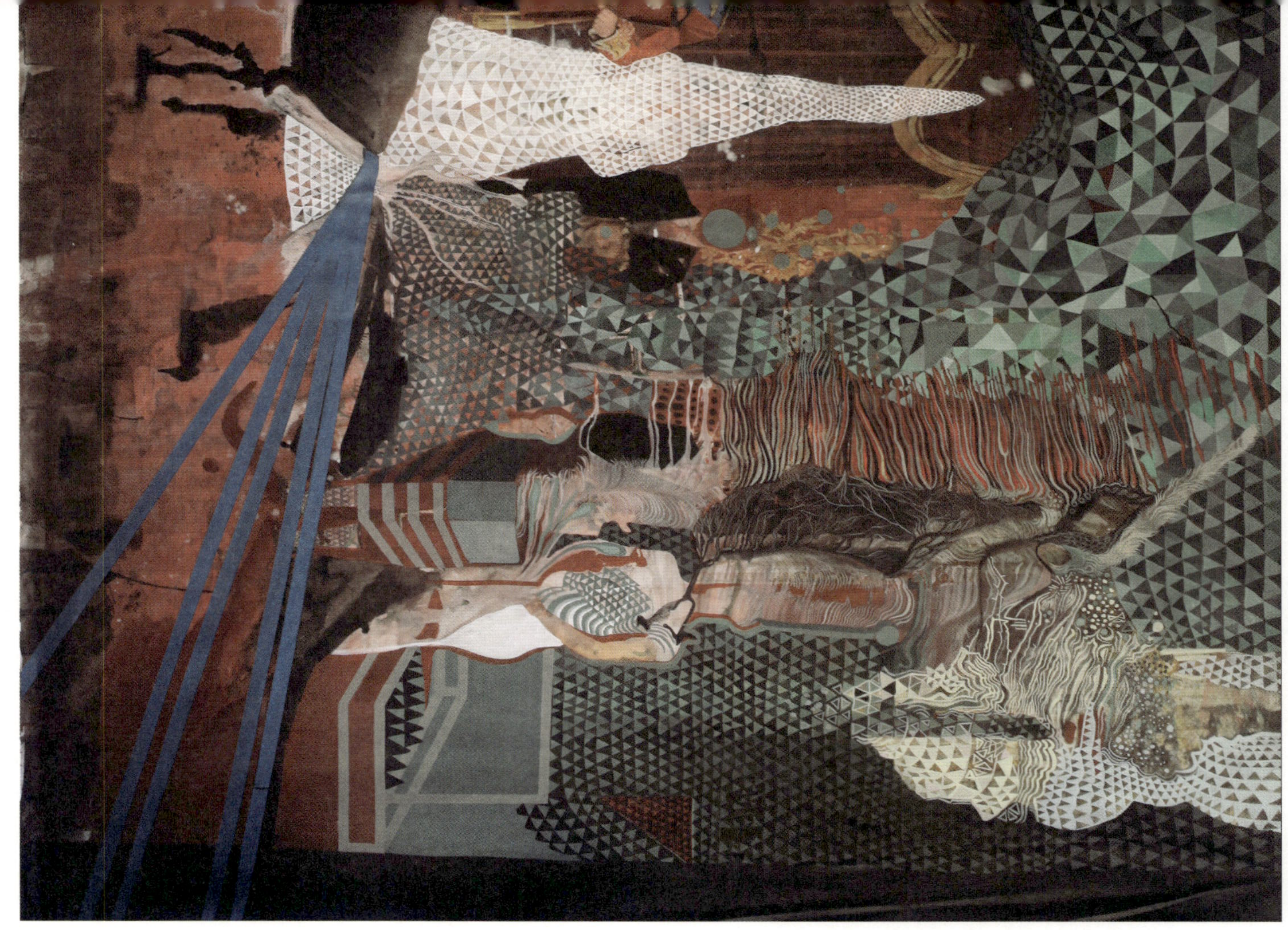

Ramin Haerizadeh, Rokni Haerizadeh and Hesam Rahmanian, *Madam Tussauds*, 2014
Acrylic on printed canvas
530 x 310 cm

XV

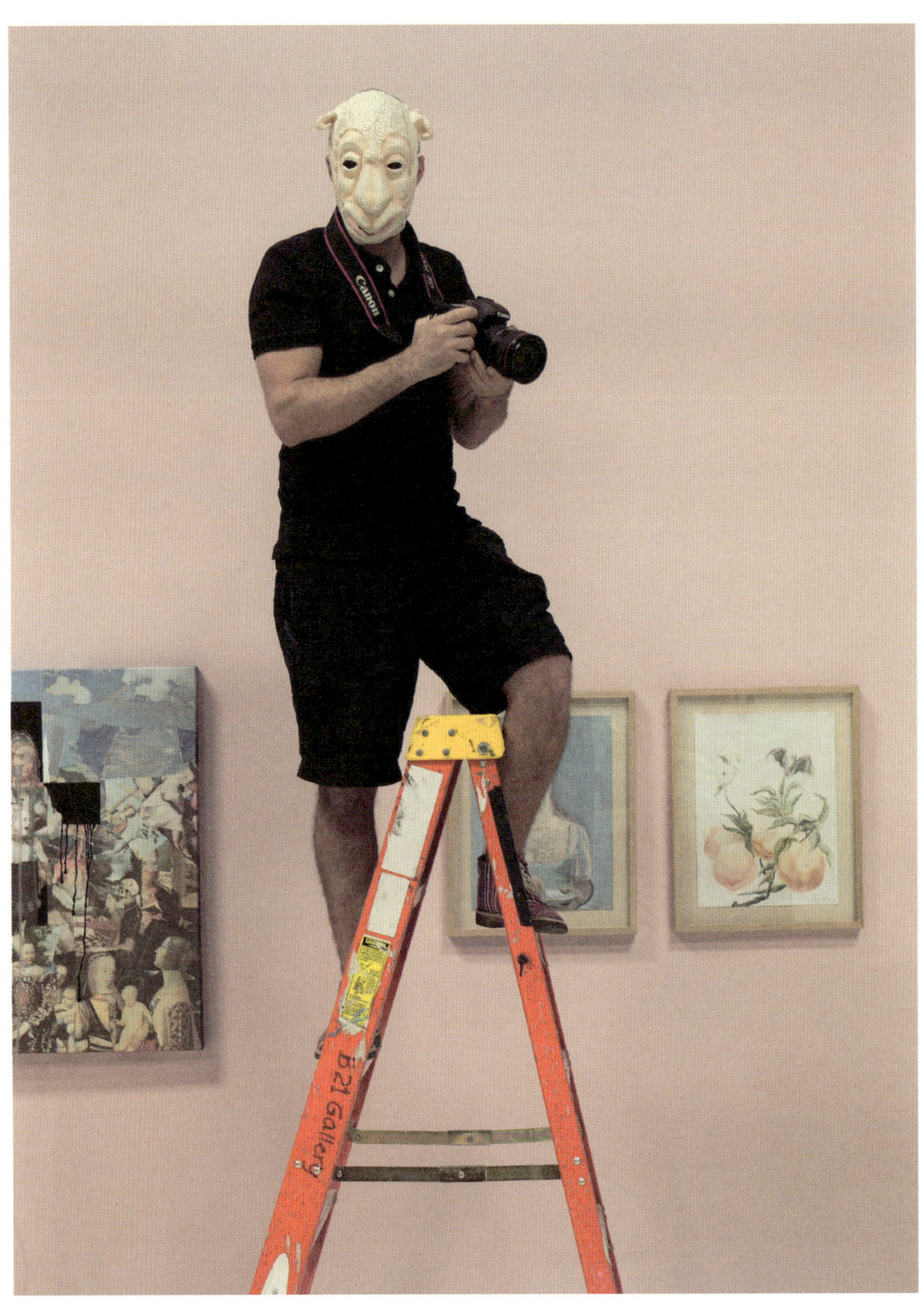

XVI

WORKS

XVII

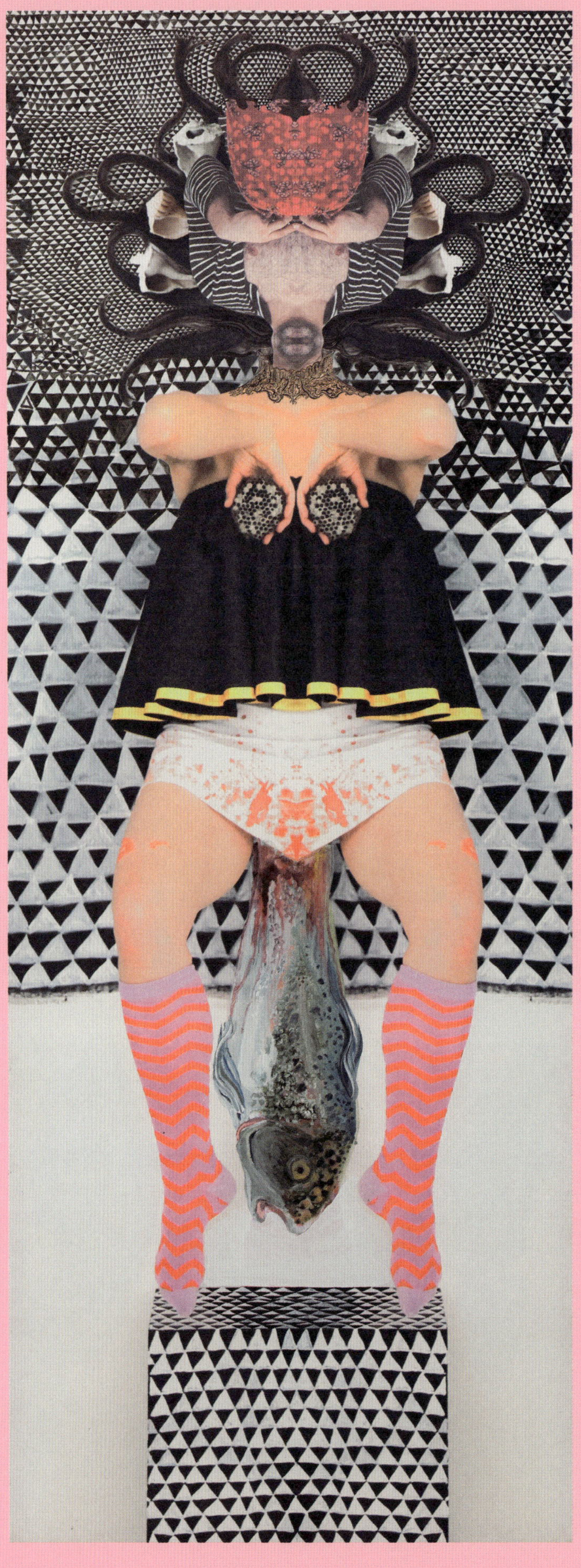

Fetish 1, 2014
Collage, acrylic and ink on printed canvas
403 x 153 cm

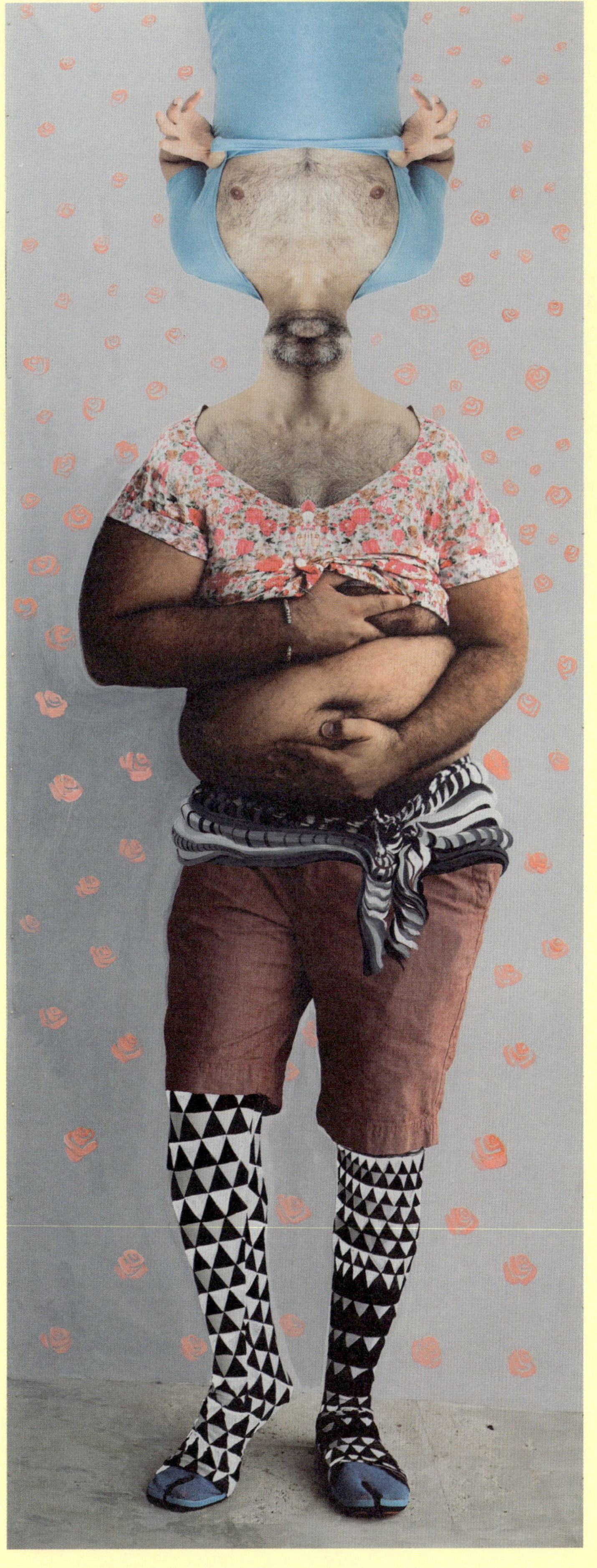

Fetish 3, 2014
Collage, acrylic and ink on printed canvas
403 x 153 cm

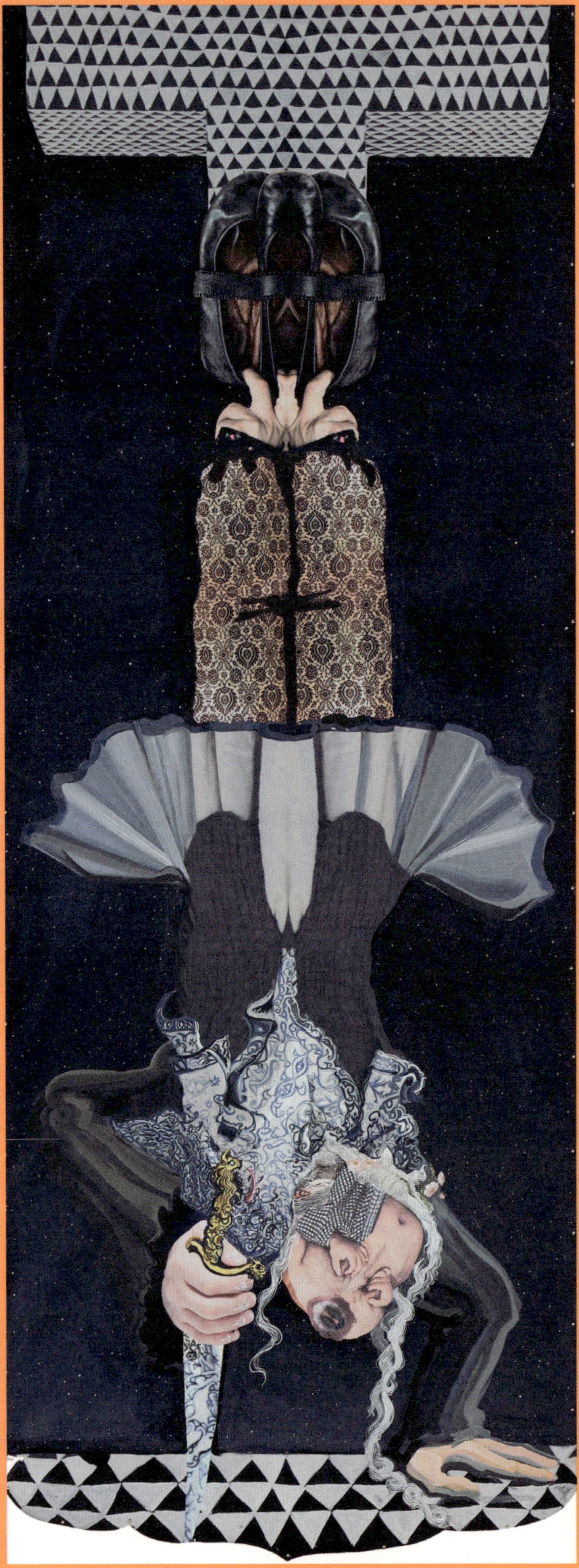

Fetish 2, 2014
Collage, acrylic and ink on printed canvas
403 x 153 cm

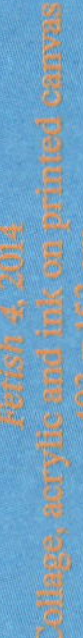

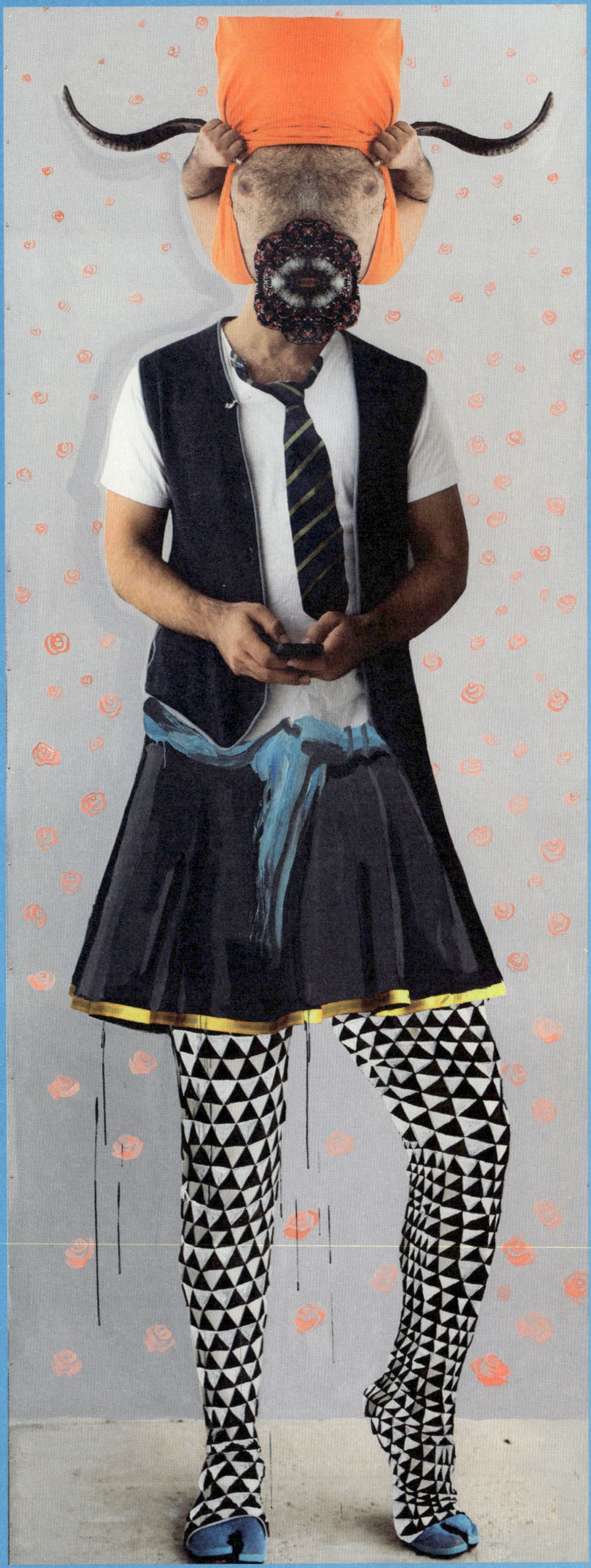

Fetish 4, 2014
Collage, acrylic and ink on printed canvas
403 x 153 cm

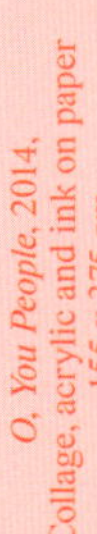

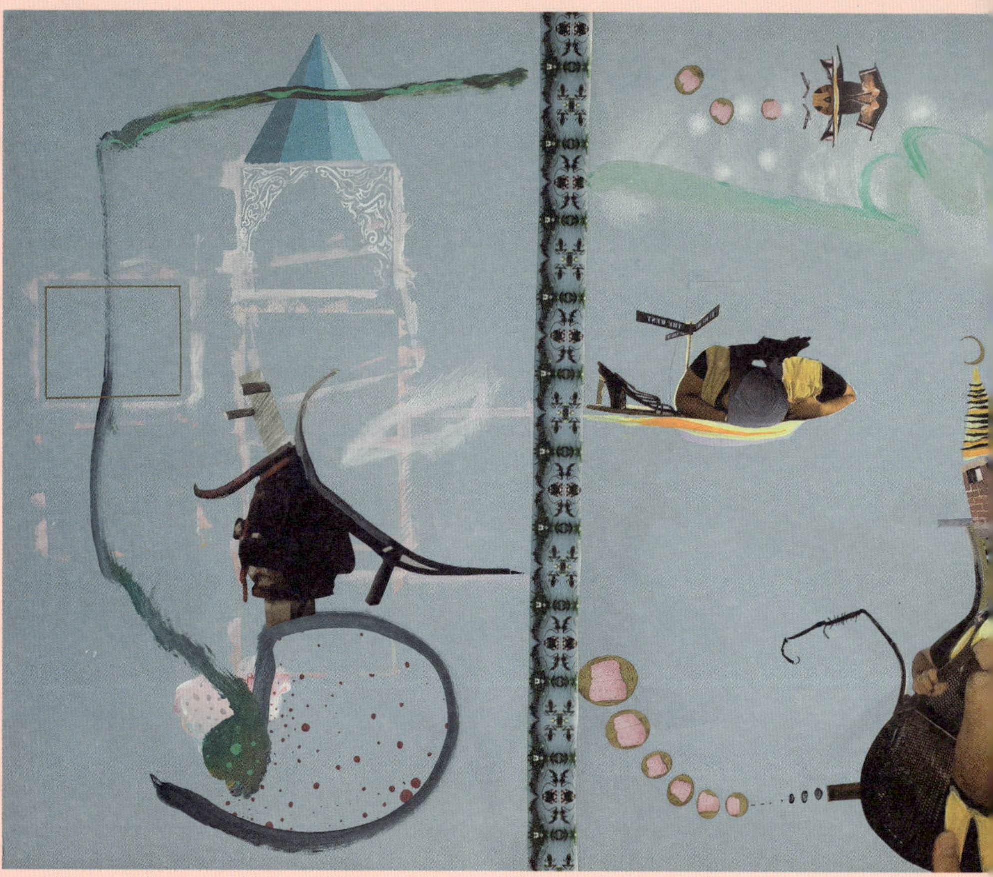

O. You People, 2014,
Collage, acrylic and ink on paper
155 x 375 cm

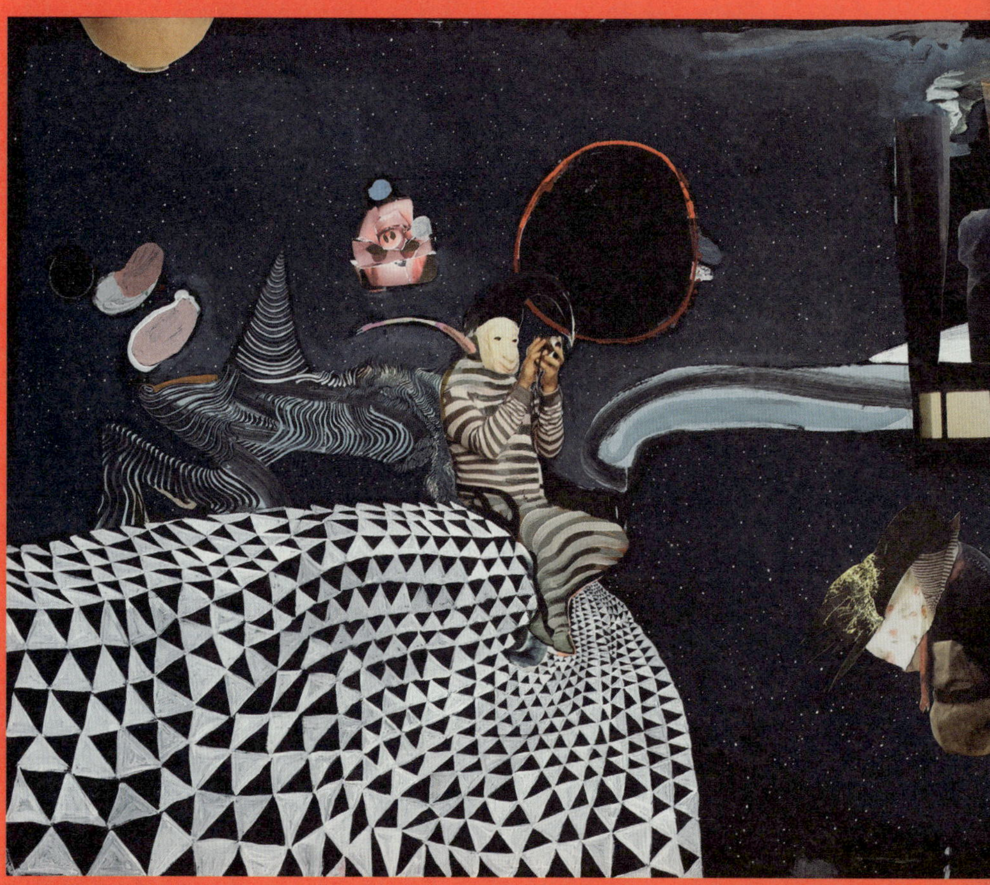

Nights of Captiva, 2014,
Collage, acrylic and ink on paper
155 x 375 cm

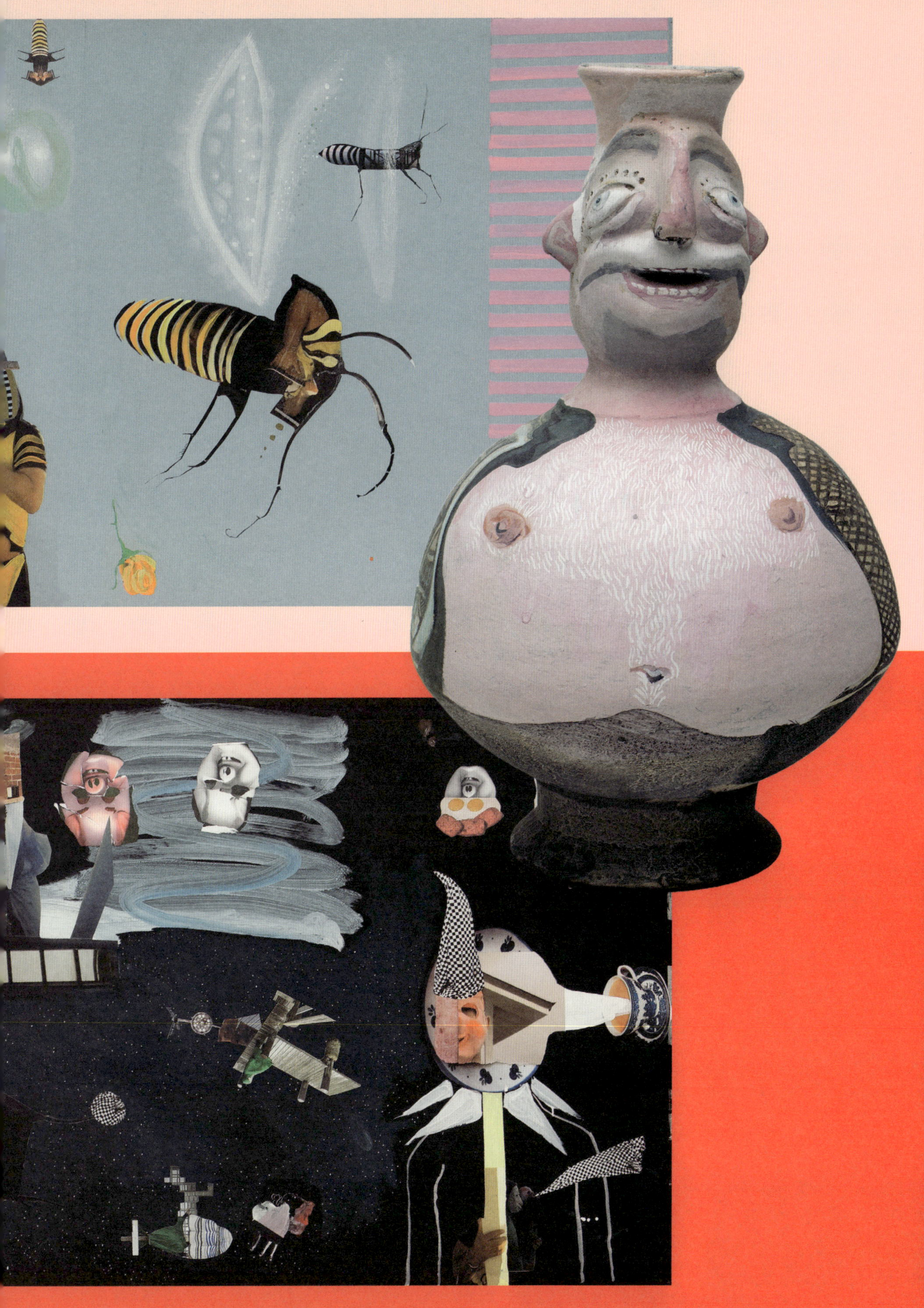

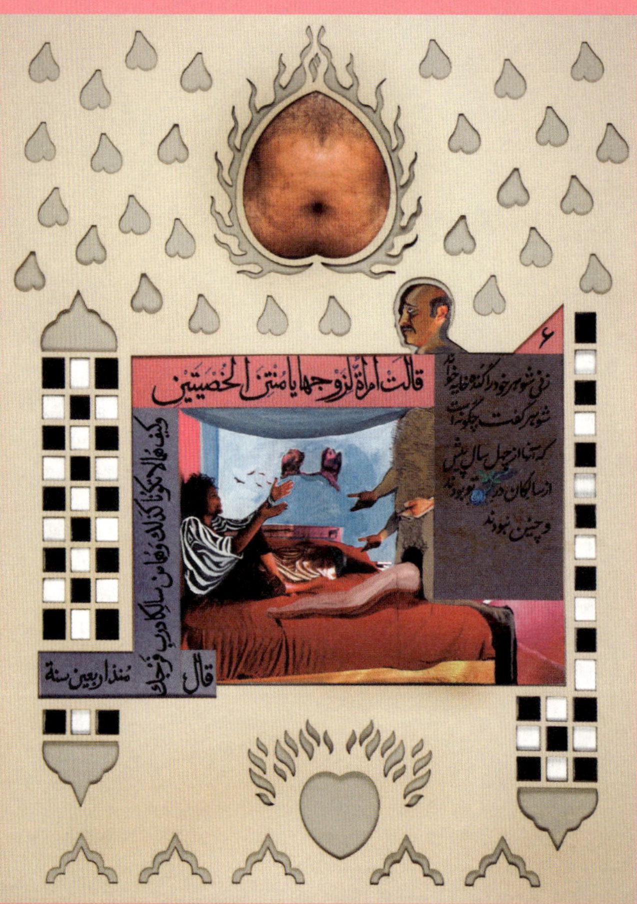

Joyous Treatise, 2011 – 2014
Collage, acrylic and ink on paper
76 x 56 cm

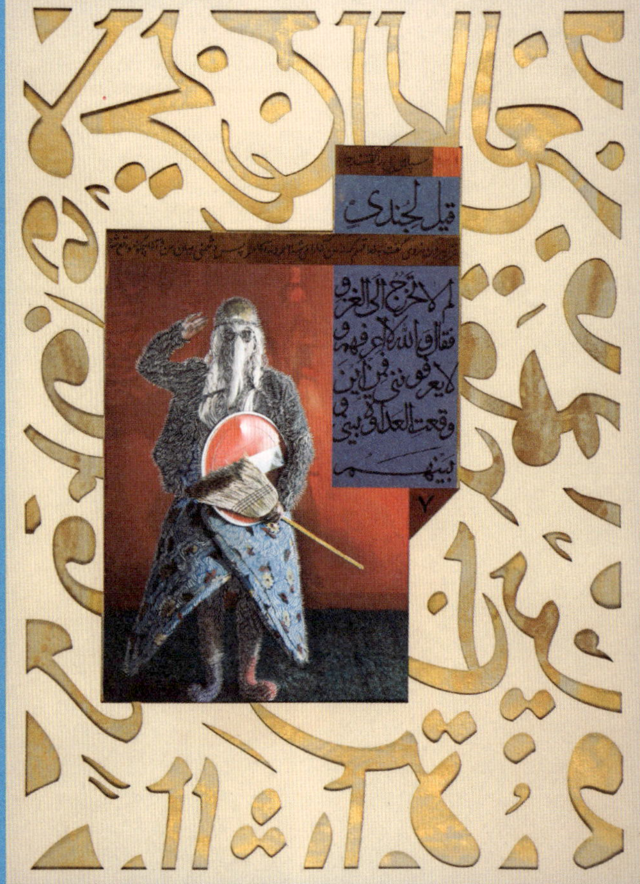

Joyous Treatise, 2011 – 2014
Collage, acrylic and ink on paper
76 x 56 cm

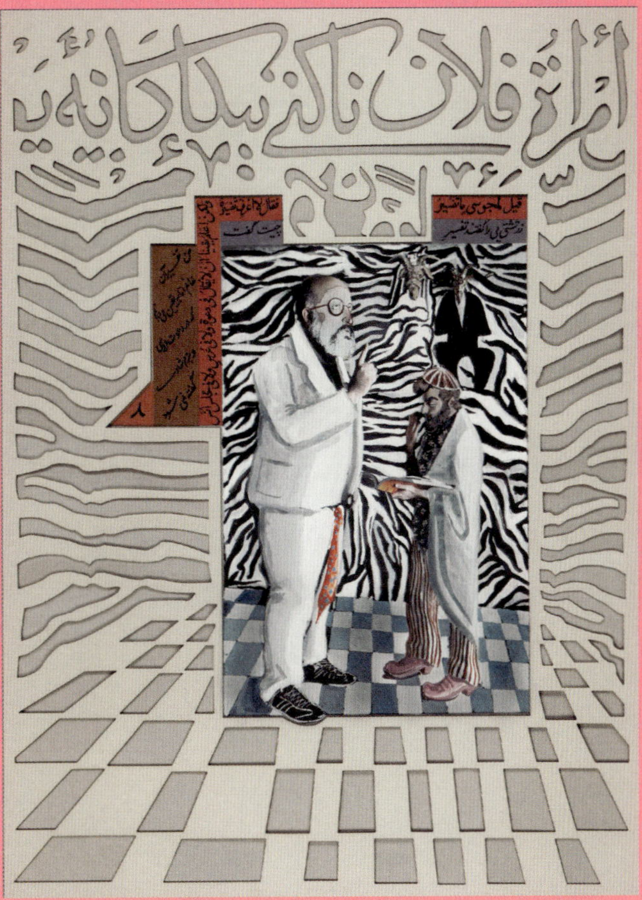

Joyous Treatise, 2011 – 2014
Collage, acrylic and ink on paper
76 x 56 cm

For translations, see pages 105 – 106

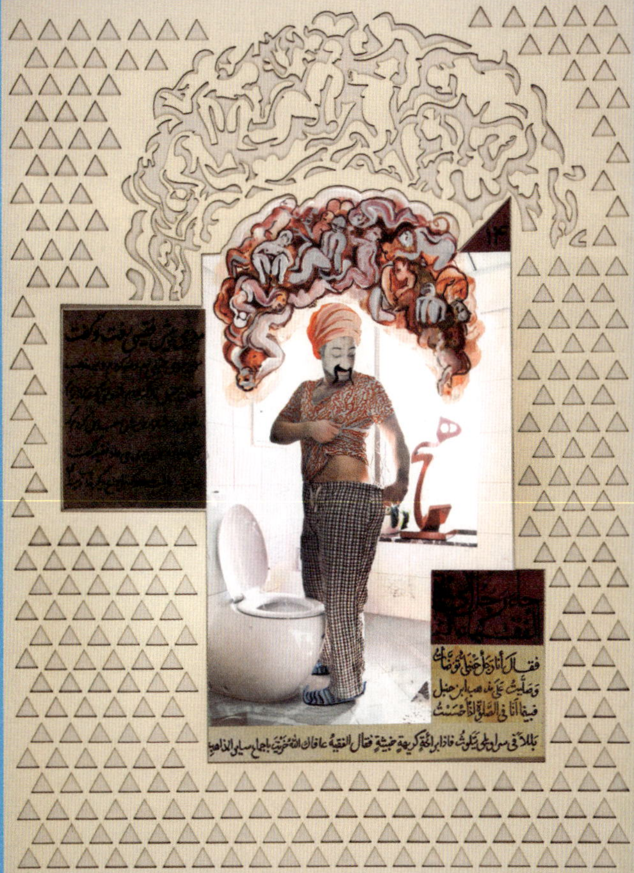

Joyous Treatise, 2011 – 2014
Collage, acrylic and ink on paper
76 x 56 cm

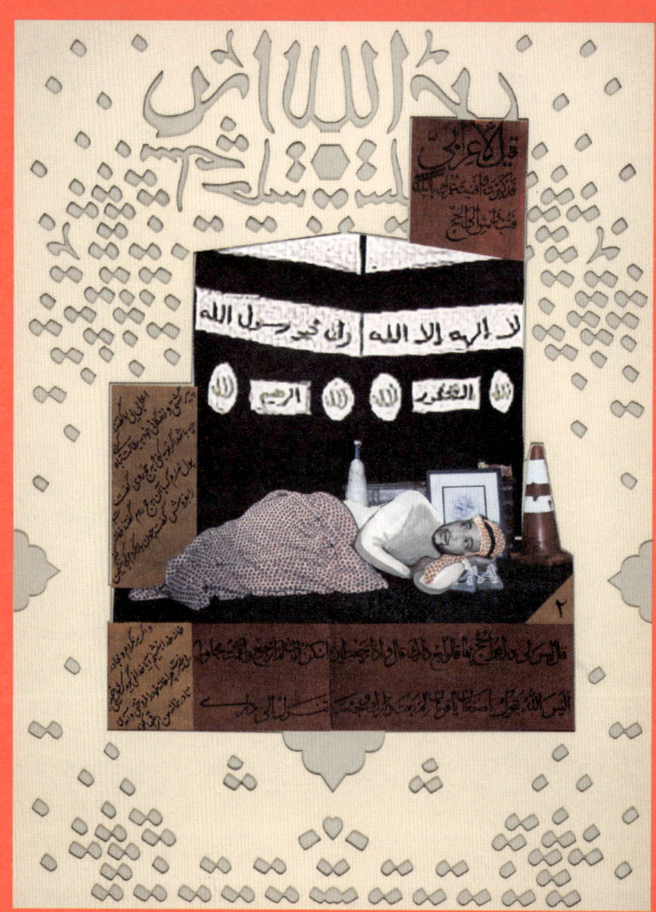

Joyous Treatise, 2011 – 2014
Collage, acrylic and ink on paper
76 x 56 cm

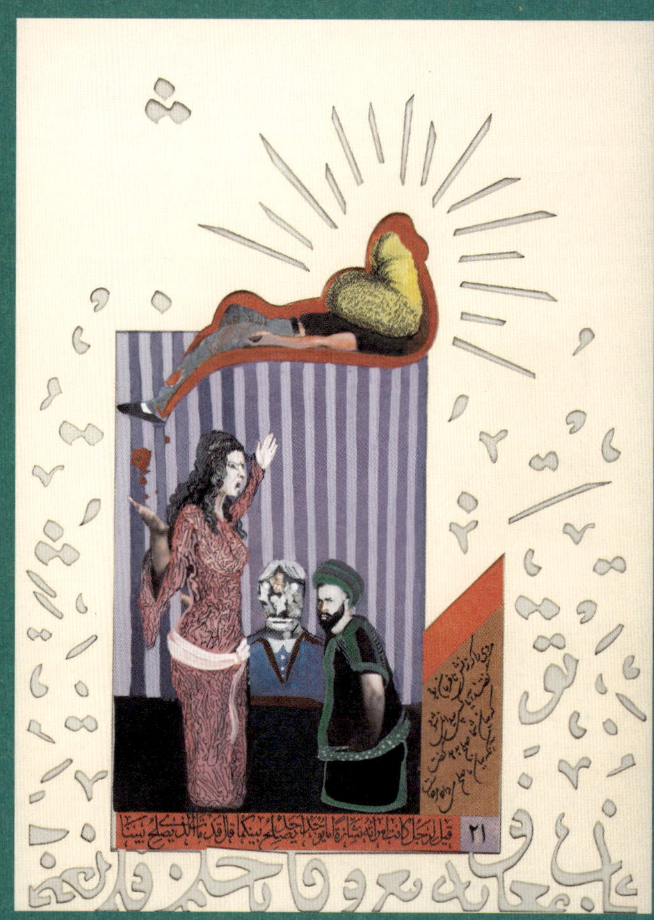

Joyous Treatise, 2011 – 2014
Collage, acrylic and ink on paper
76 x 56 cm

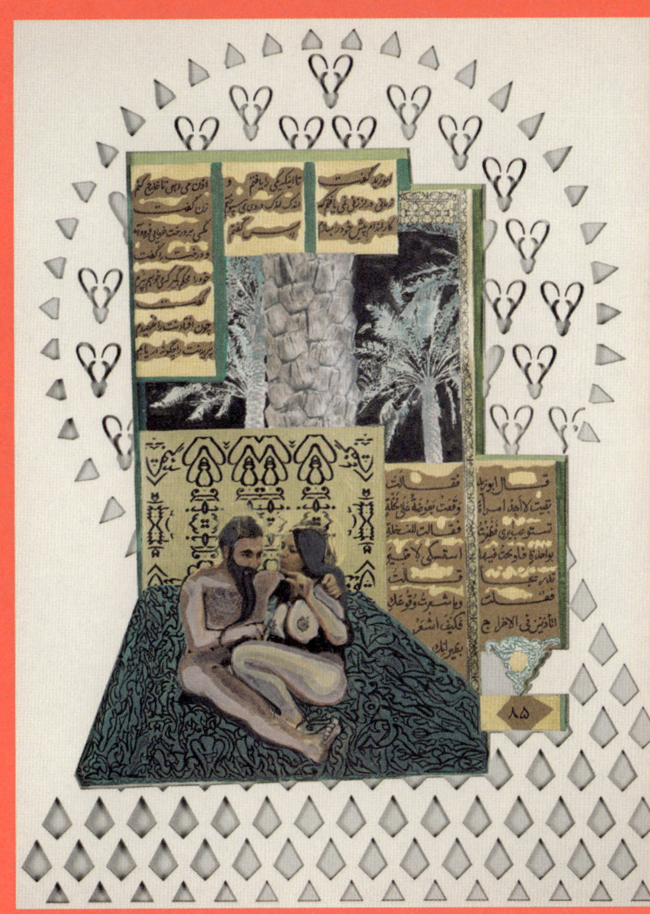

For translations, see pages 105 – 106

Joyous Treatise, 2011 – 2014
Collage, acrylic and ink on paper
76 x 56 cm

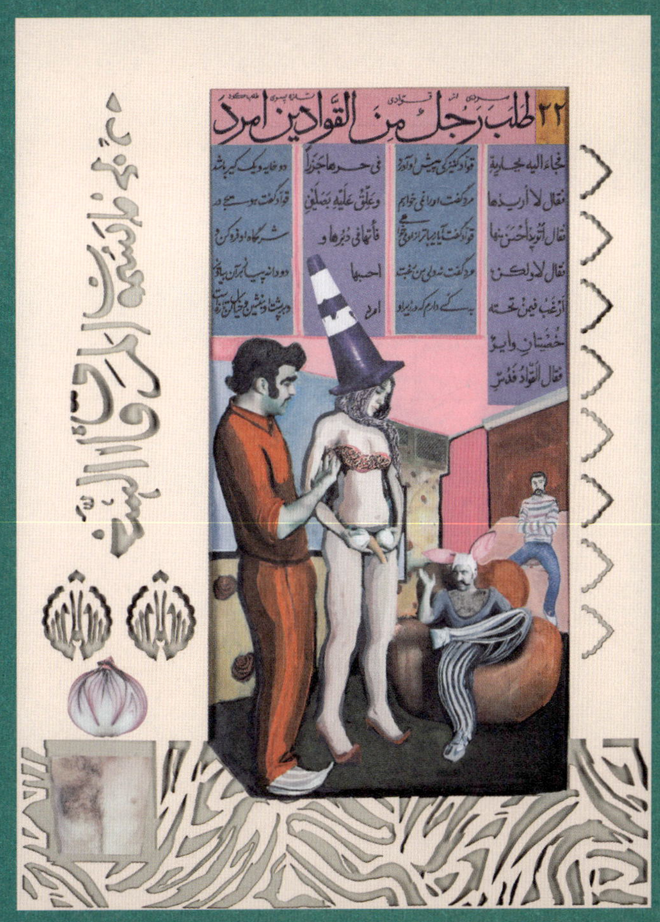

Joyous Treatise, 2011 – 2014
Collage, acrylic and ink on paper
76 x 56 cm

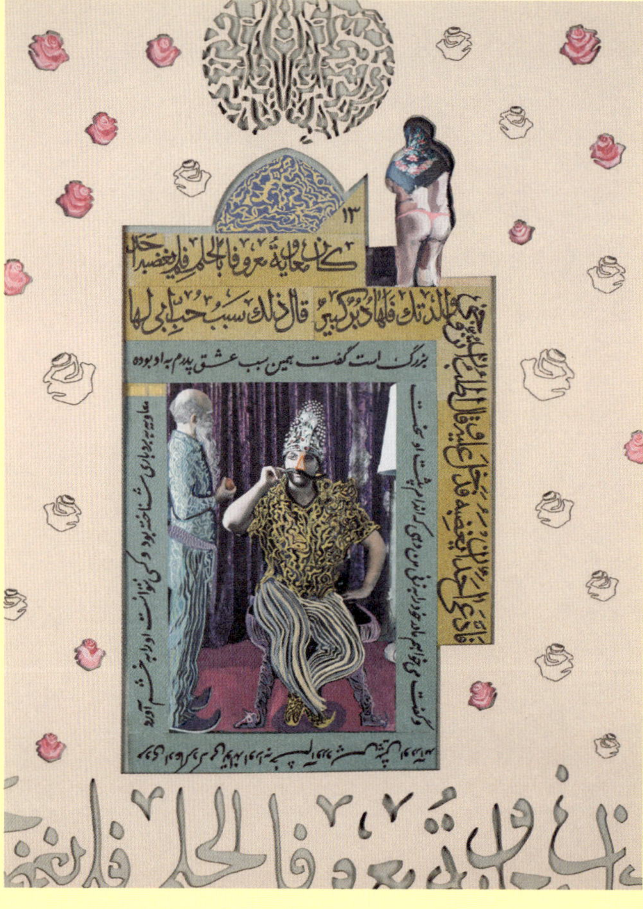

Joyous Treatise, 2011 – 2014
Collage, acrylic and ink on paper
76 x 56 cm

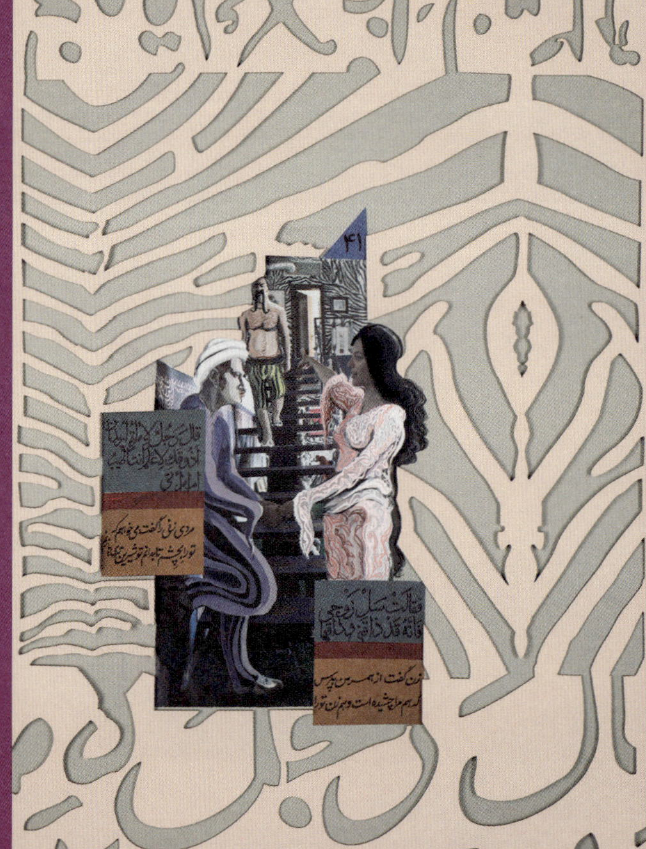

Joyous Treatise, 2011 – 2014
Collage, acrylic and ink on paper
76 x 56 cm

For translations, see pages 105 – 106

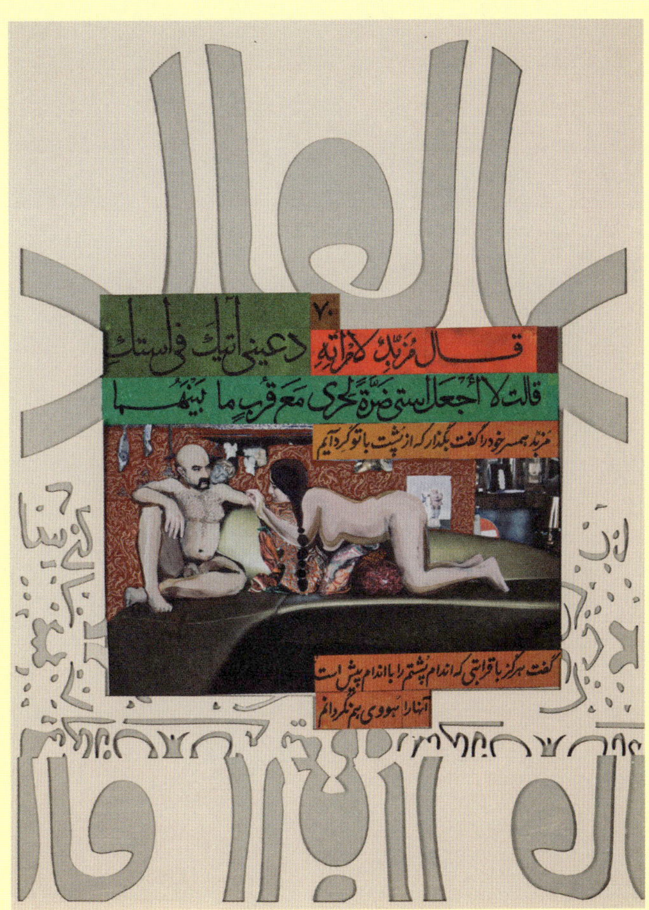

Joyous Treatise, 2011 – 2014
Collage, acrylic and ink on paper
76 x 56 cm

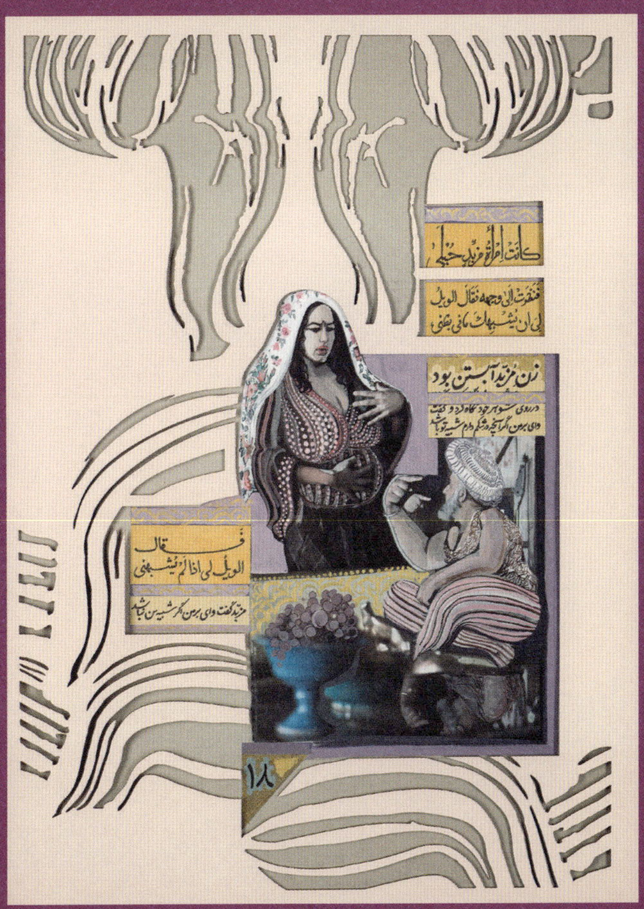

Joyous Treatise, 2011 – 2014
Collage, acrylic and ink on paper
76 x 56 cm

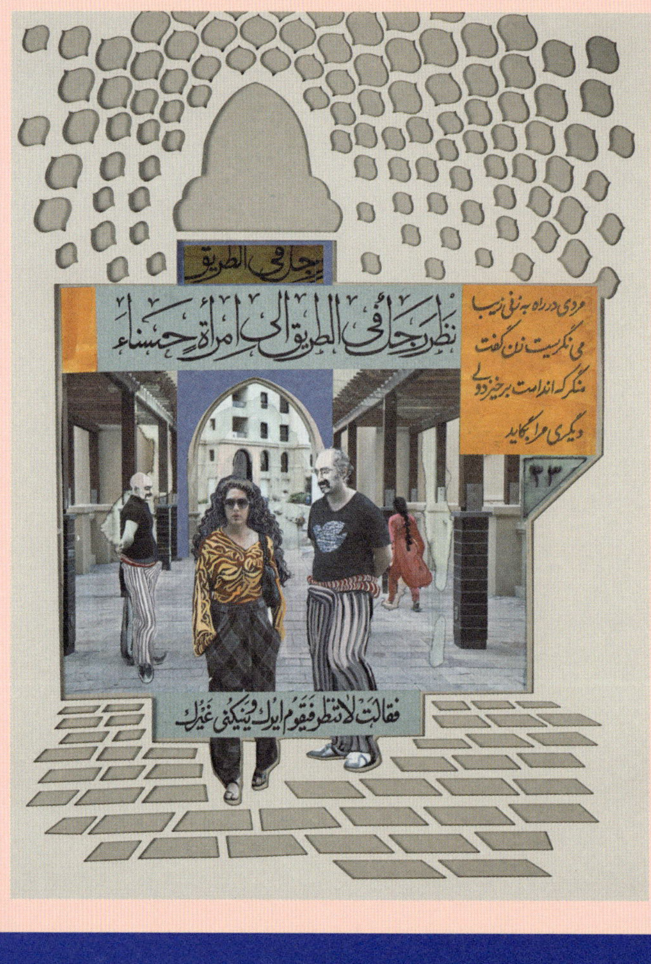

Joyous Treatise, 2011 – 2014
Collage, acrylic and ink on paper
76 x 56 cm

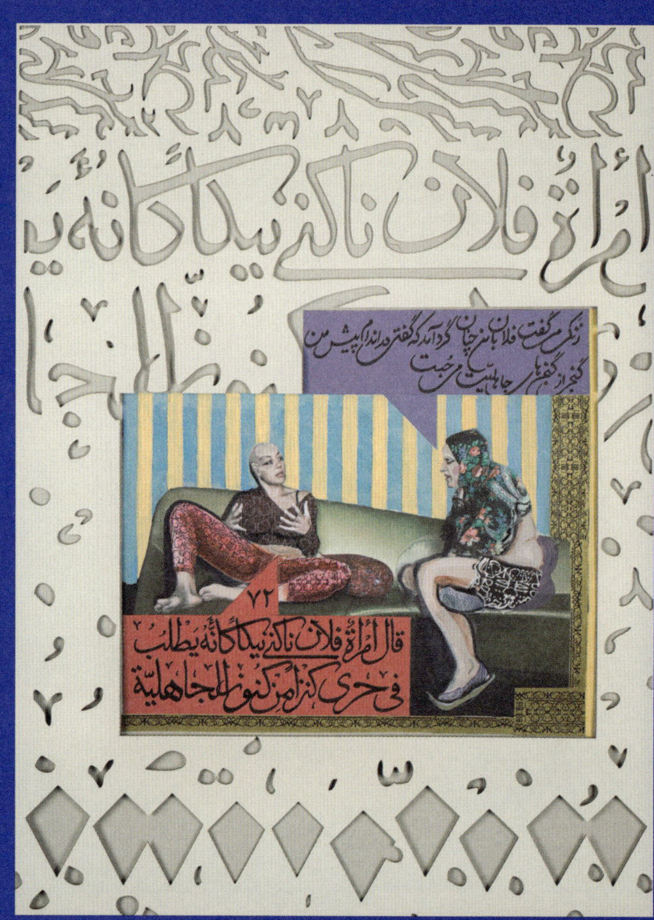

Joyous Treatise, 2011 – 2014
Collage, acrylic and ink on paper
76 x 56 cm

For translations, see pages 105 – 106

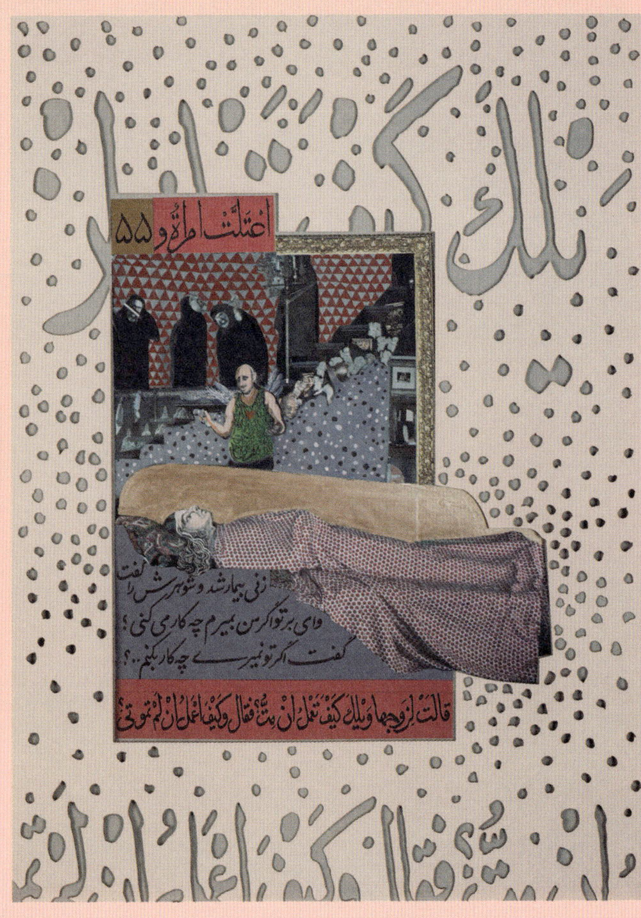

Joyous Treatise, 2011 – 2014
Collage, acrylic and ink on paper
76 x 56 cm

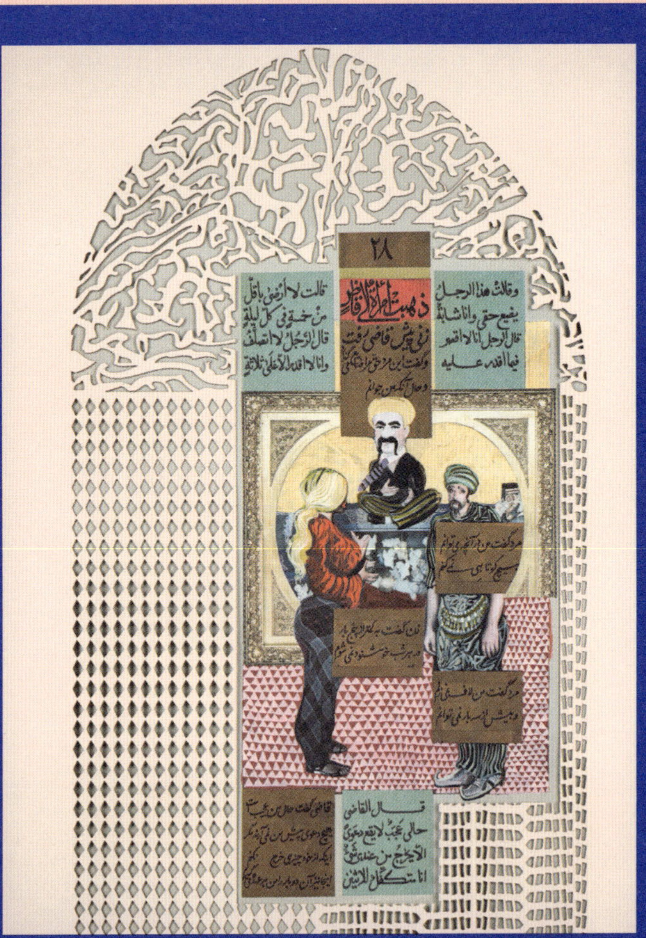

Joyous Treatise, 2011 – 2014
Collage, acrylic and ink on paper
76 x 56 cm

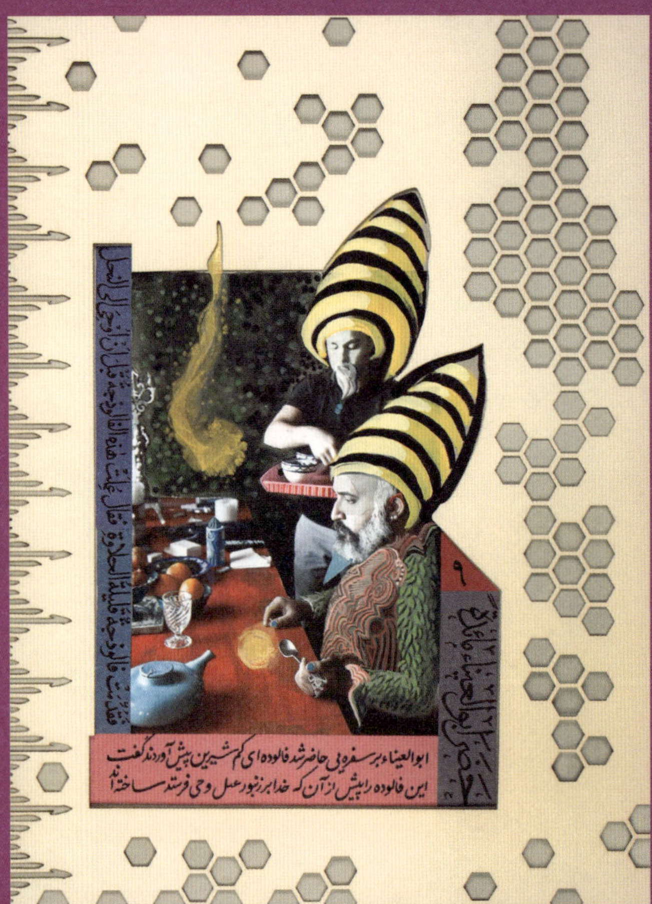

Joyous Treatise, 2011 – 2014
Collage, acrylic and ink on paper
76 x 56 cm

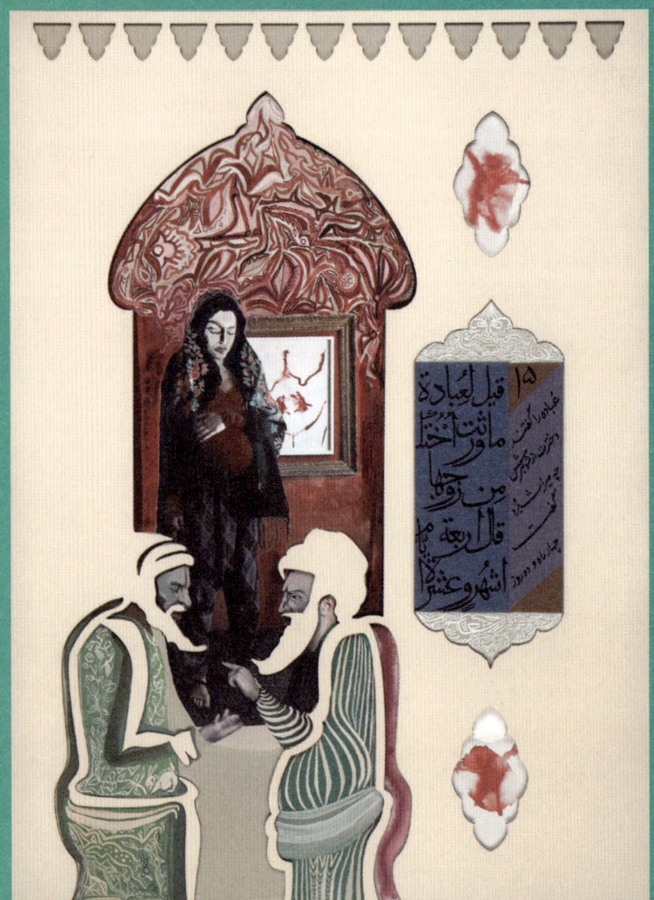

Joyous Treatise, 2011 – 2014
Collage, acrylic and ink on paper
76 x 56 cm

For translations, see pages 105 – 106

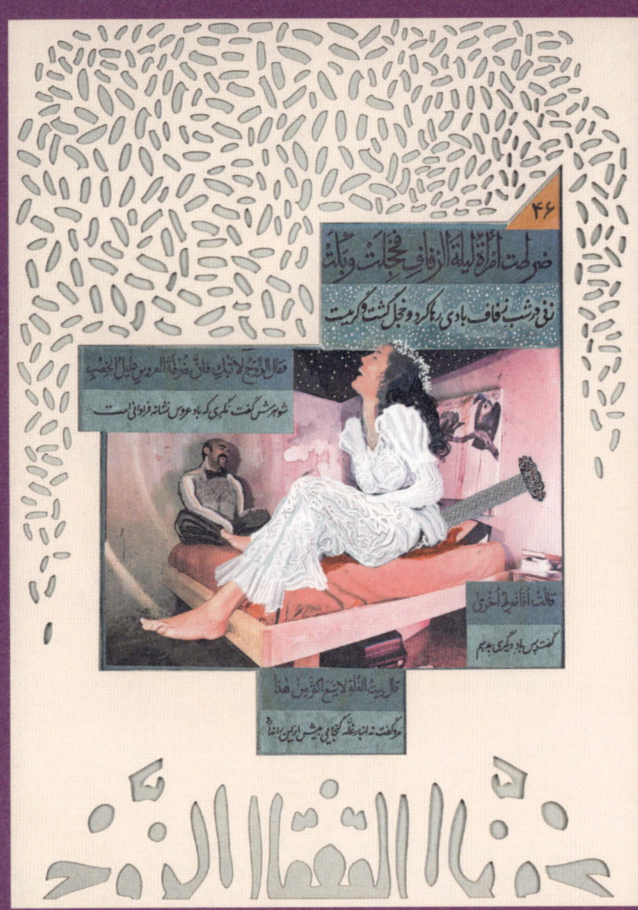

Joyous Treatise, 2001 – 2014
Collage, acrylic and ink on paper
76 x 56 cm

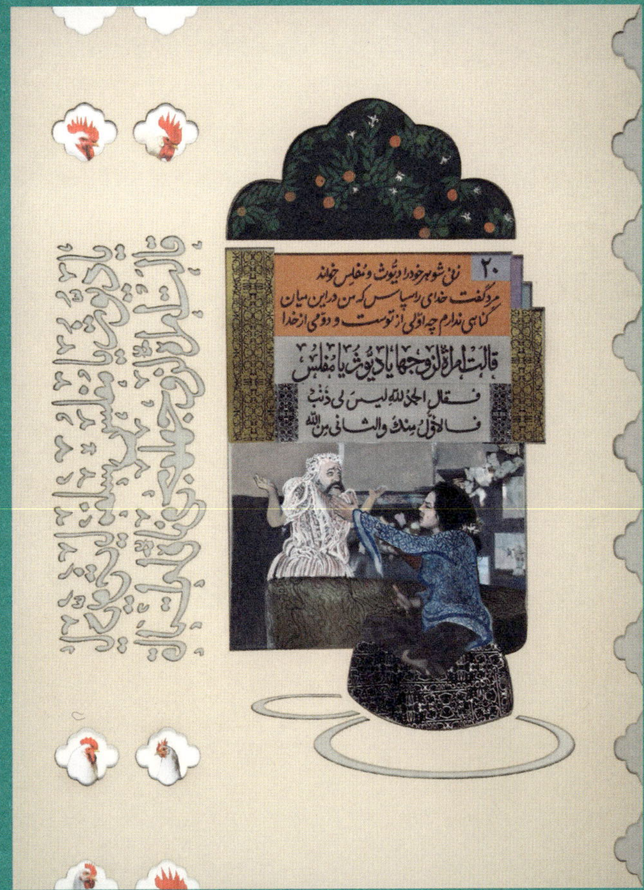

Joyous Treatise, 2001 – 2014
Collage, acrylic and ink on paper
76 x 56 cm

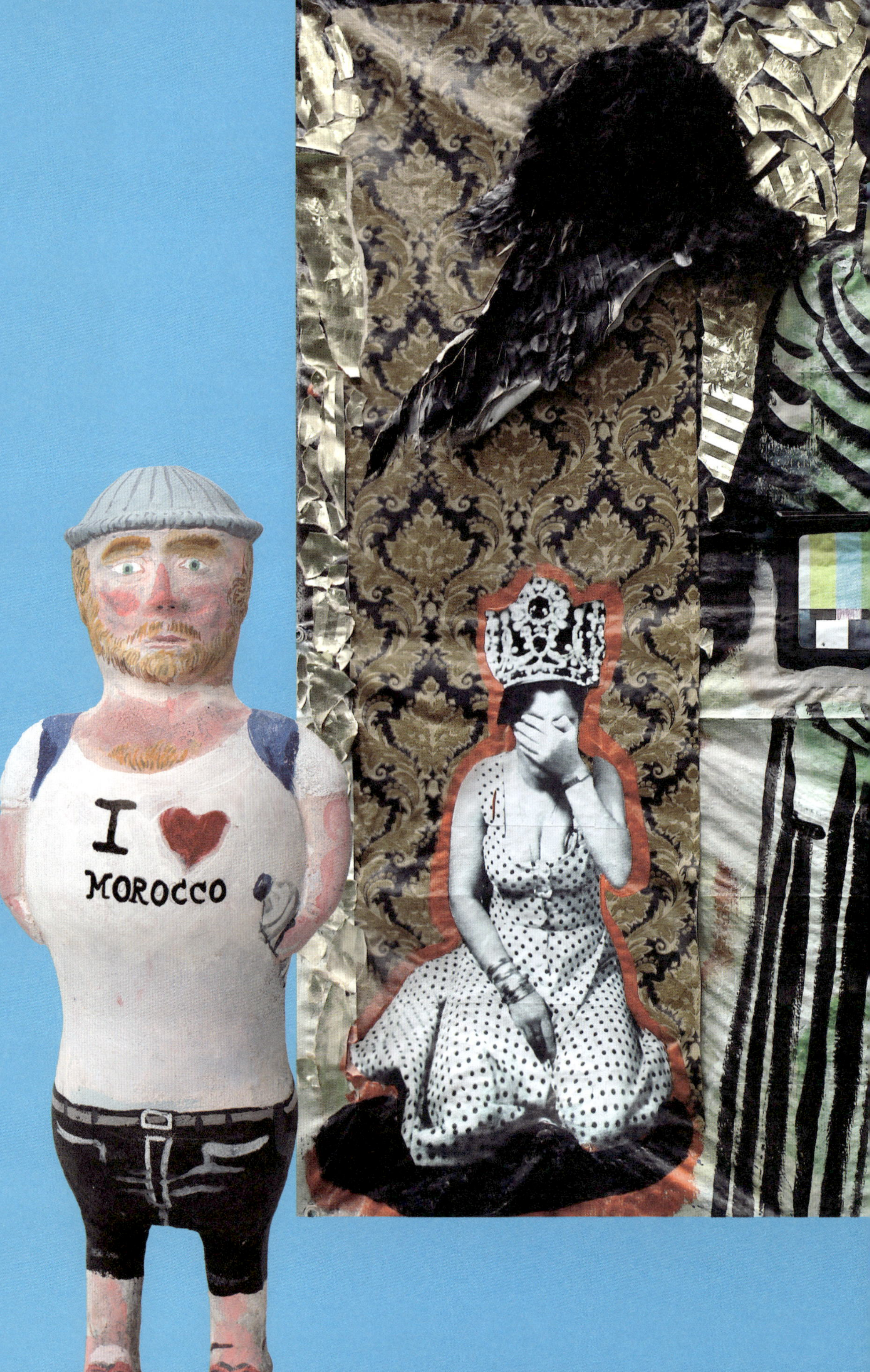

Garden of Grandmothers 09, 2012
Feathers, paper collage, acrylic and wallpaper on plastic tarp
185 x 240 cm

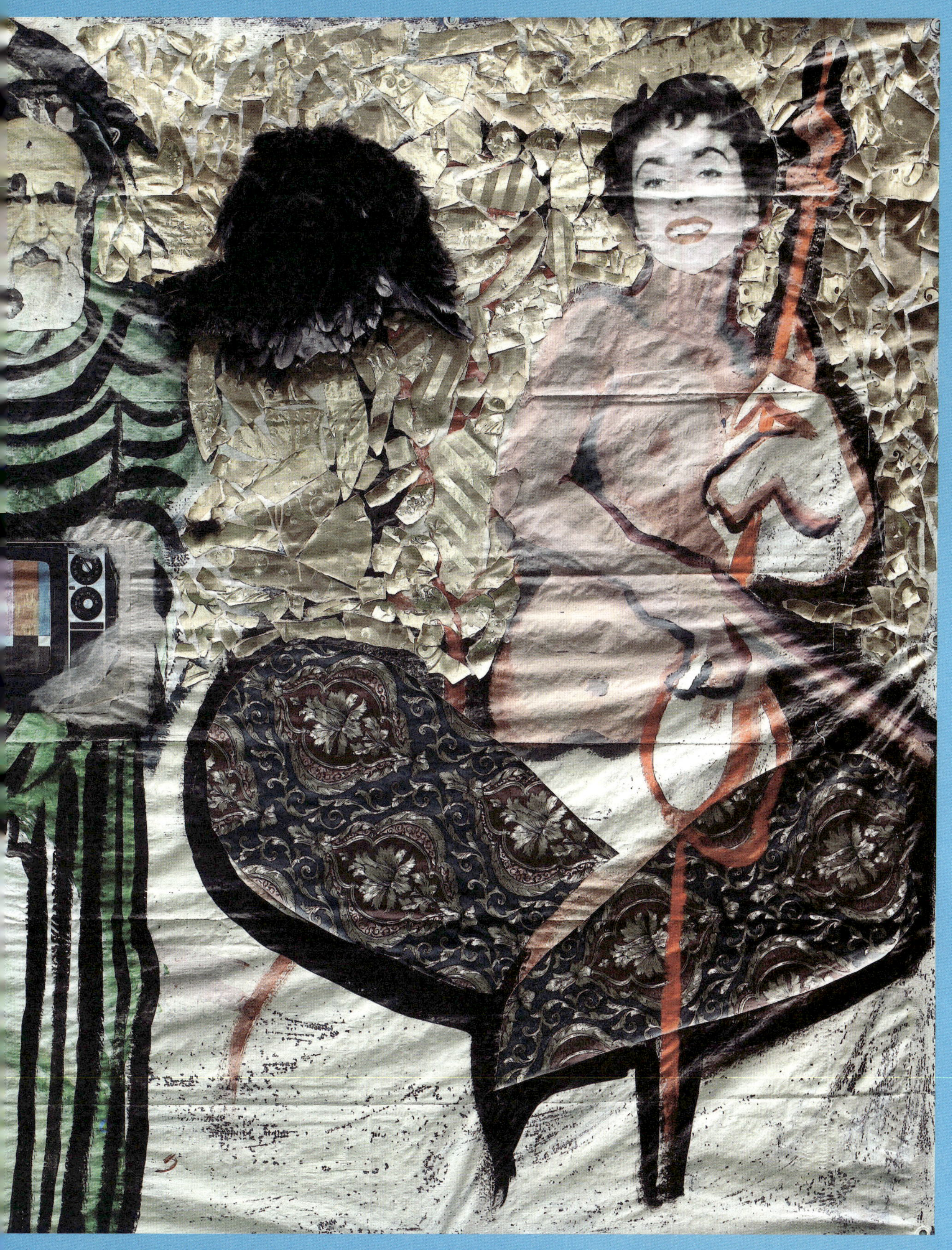

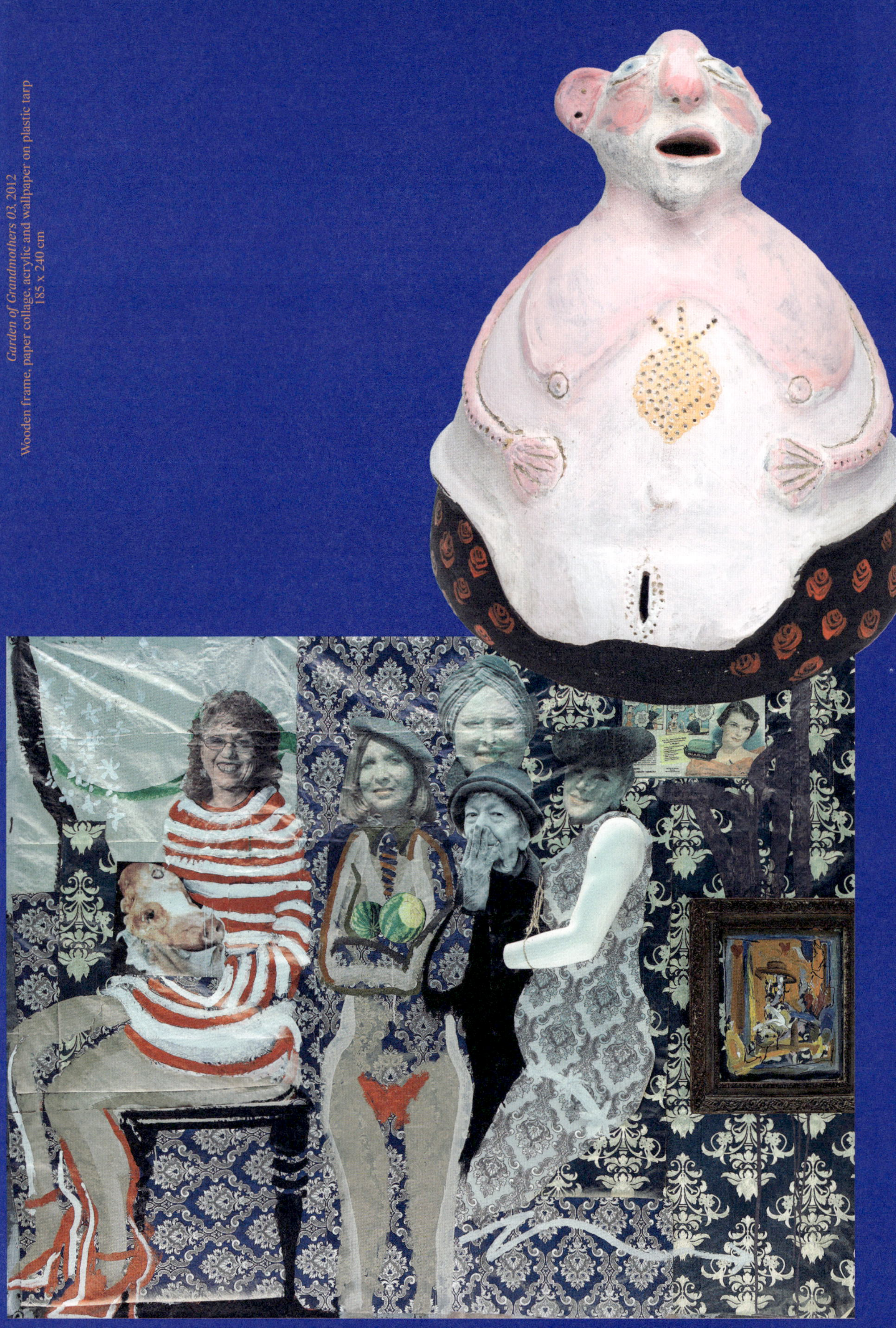

Garden of Grandmothers 03, 2012
Wooden frame, paper collage, acrylic and wallpaper on plastic tarp
185 x 240 cm

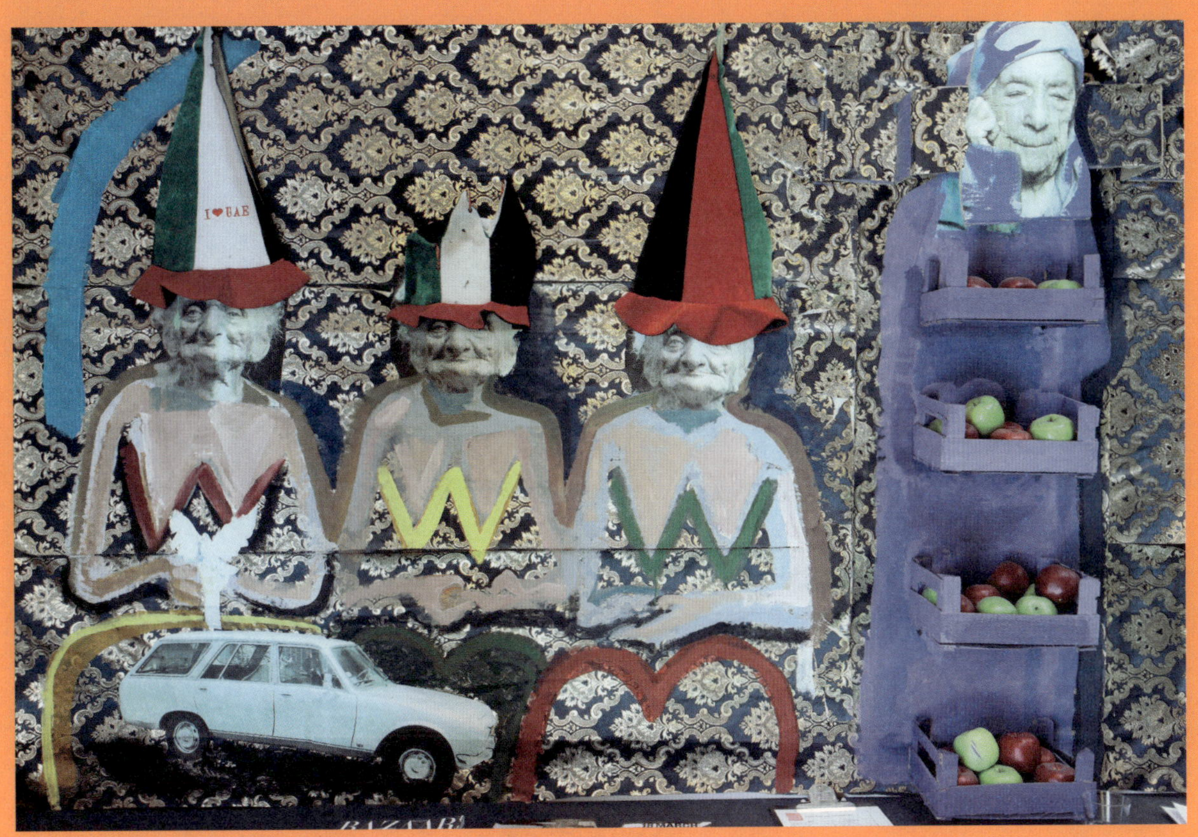

Garden of Grandmothers 02, 2012
Wooden fruit boxes, plastic fruits, readymade hats, wallpaper, acrylic
and paper collage on plastic tarp
153 x 244 x 20 cm

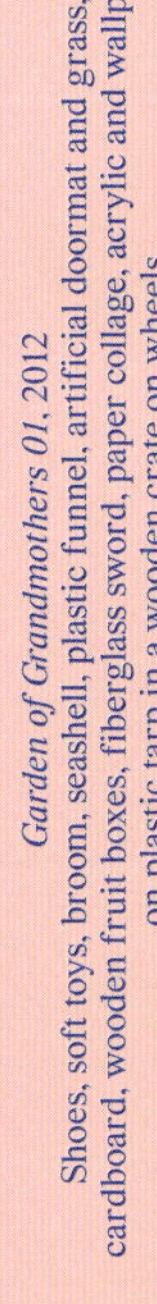

Garden of Grandmothers 01, 2012
Shoes, soft toys, broom, seashell, plastic funnel, artificial doormat and grass,
cardboard, wooden fruit boxes, fiberglass sword, paper collage, acrylic and wallpaper
on plastic tarp in a wooden crate on wheels
185 x 240 x 40 cm

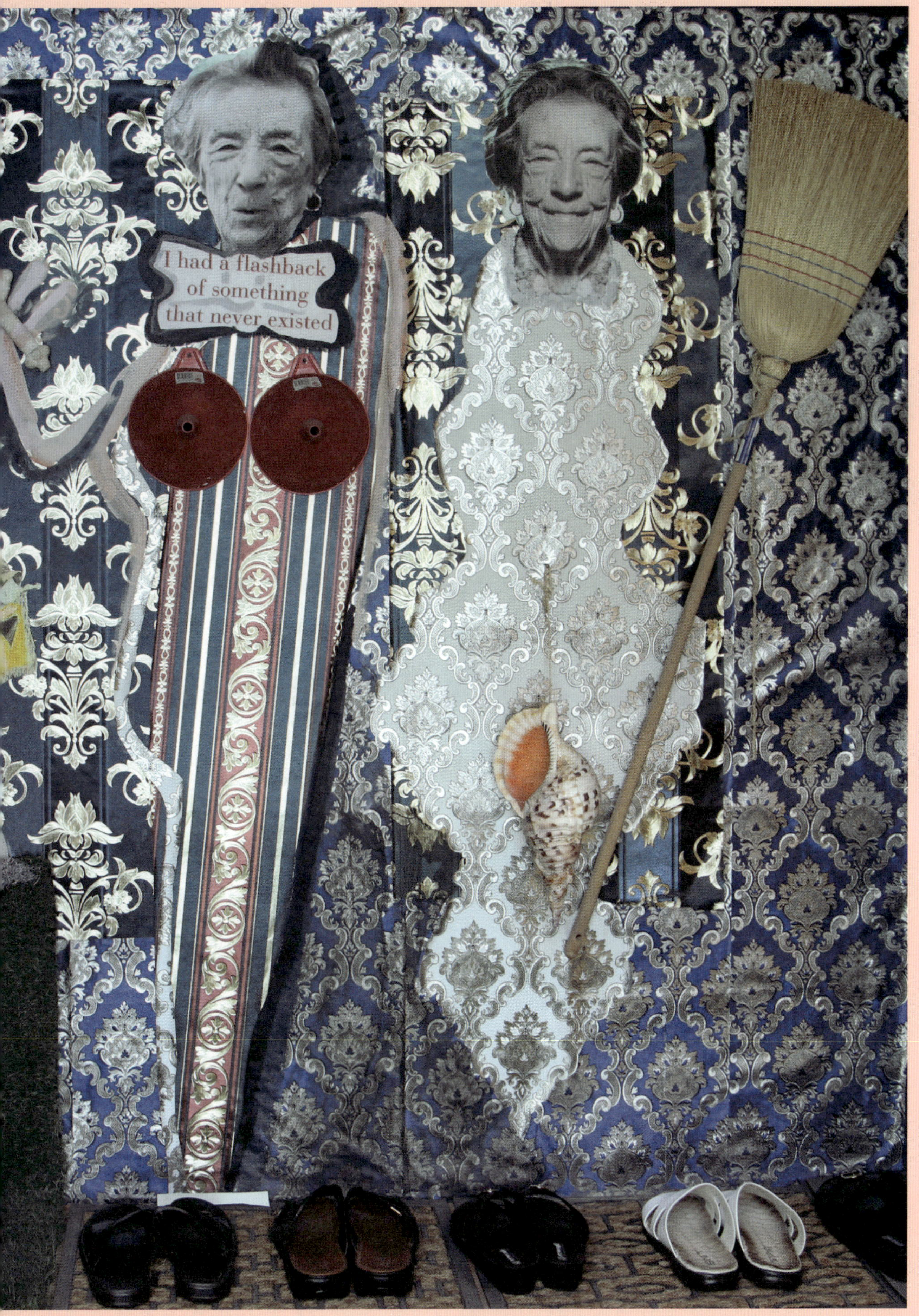

I had a flashback
of something
that never existed

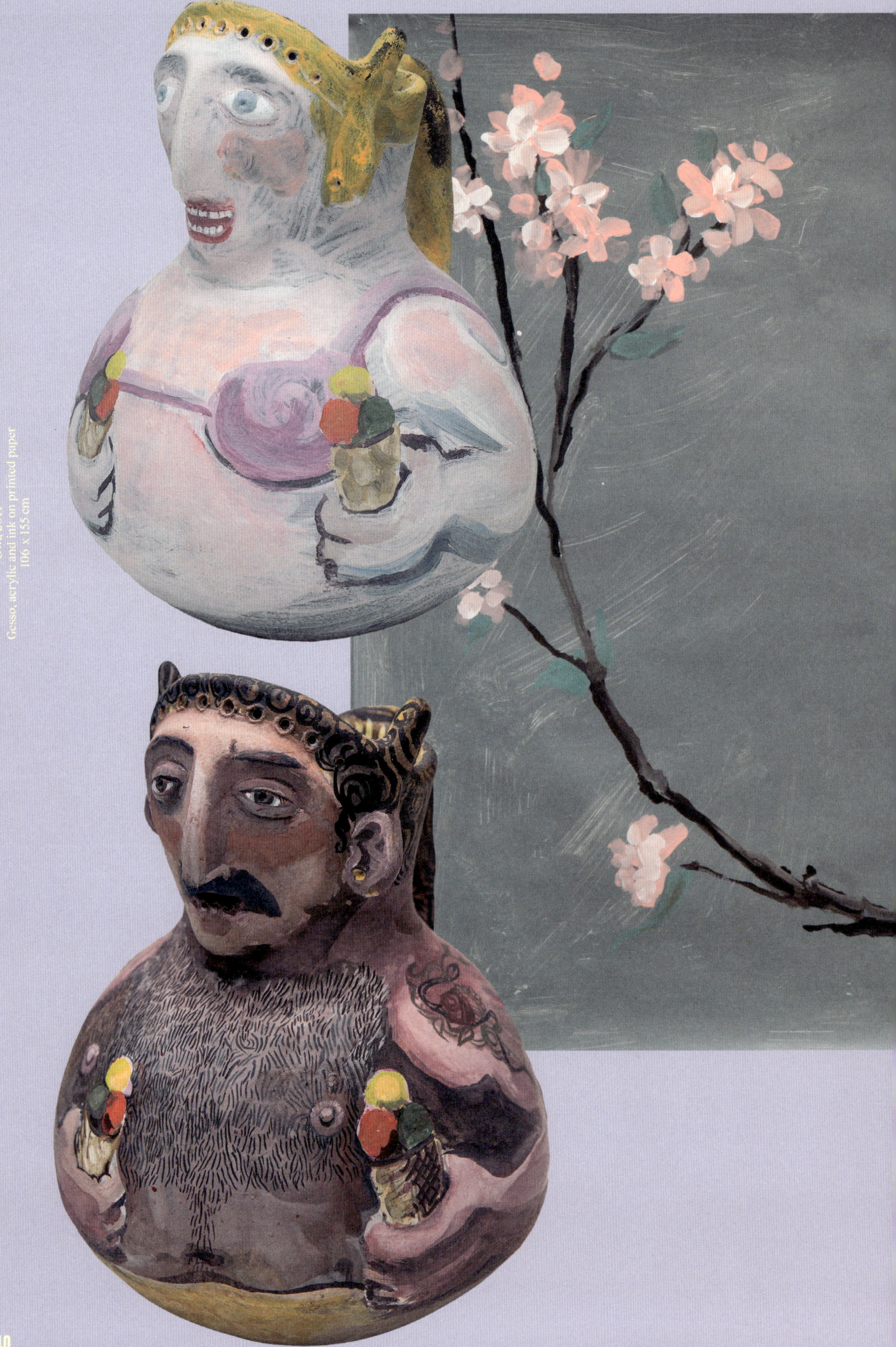

Owl, 2014
Gesso, acrylic and ink on printed paper
106 x 155 cm

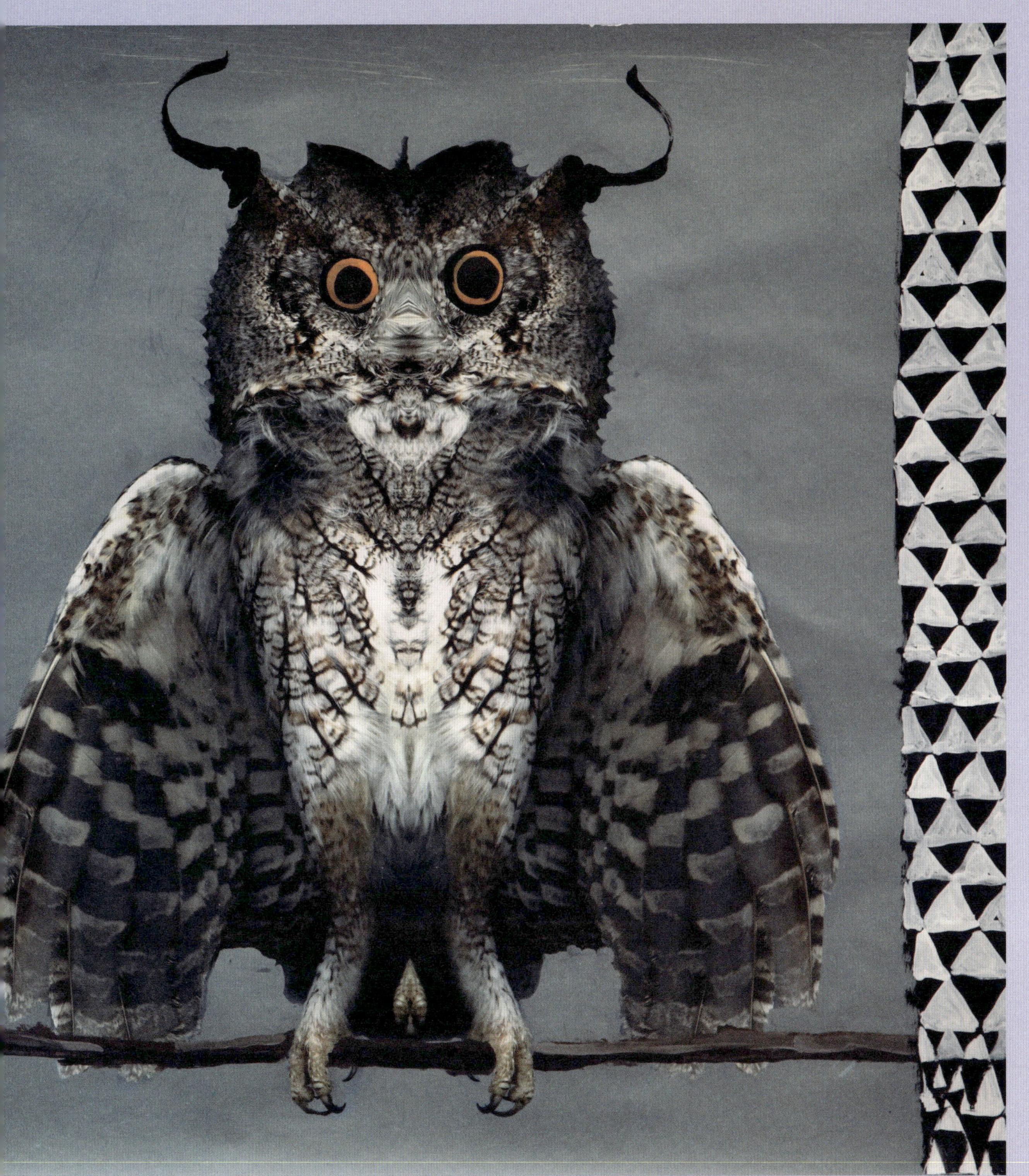

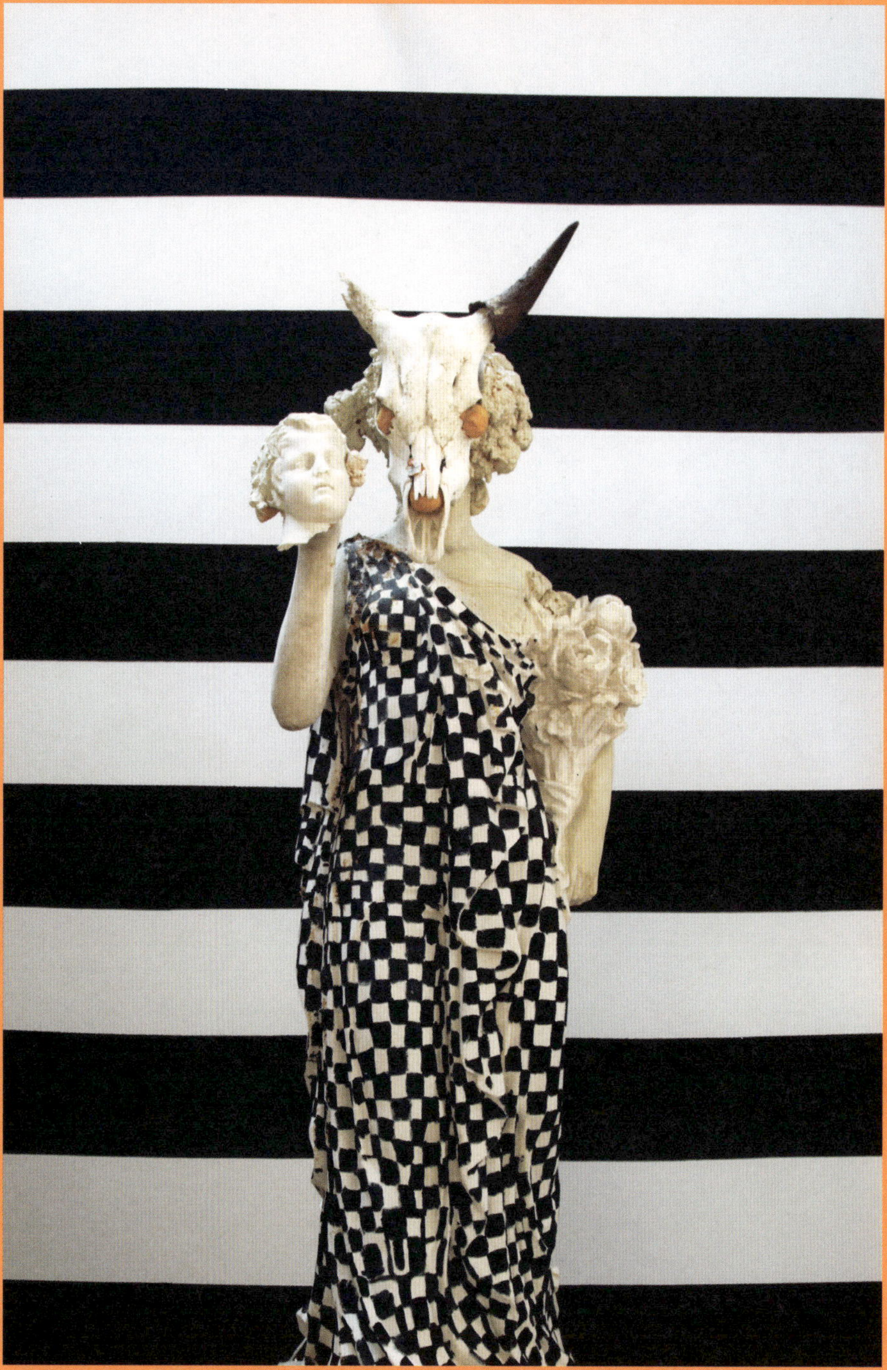

Balzac, 2012
Stone powder readymade sculpture, cow skull, foam, fibreglass sculpture, modelling paste, acrylic paint, fibreglass mannequin body part
243 x 80 x 55 cm

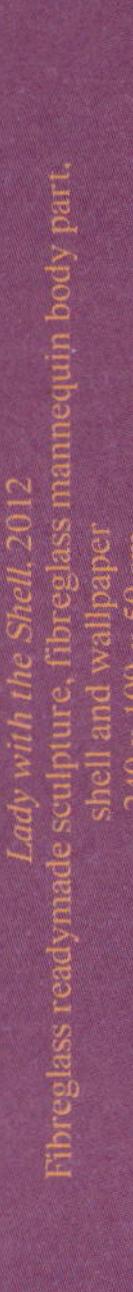

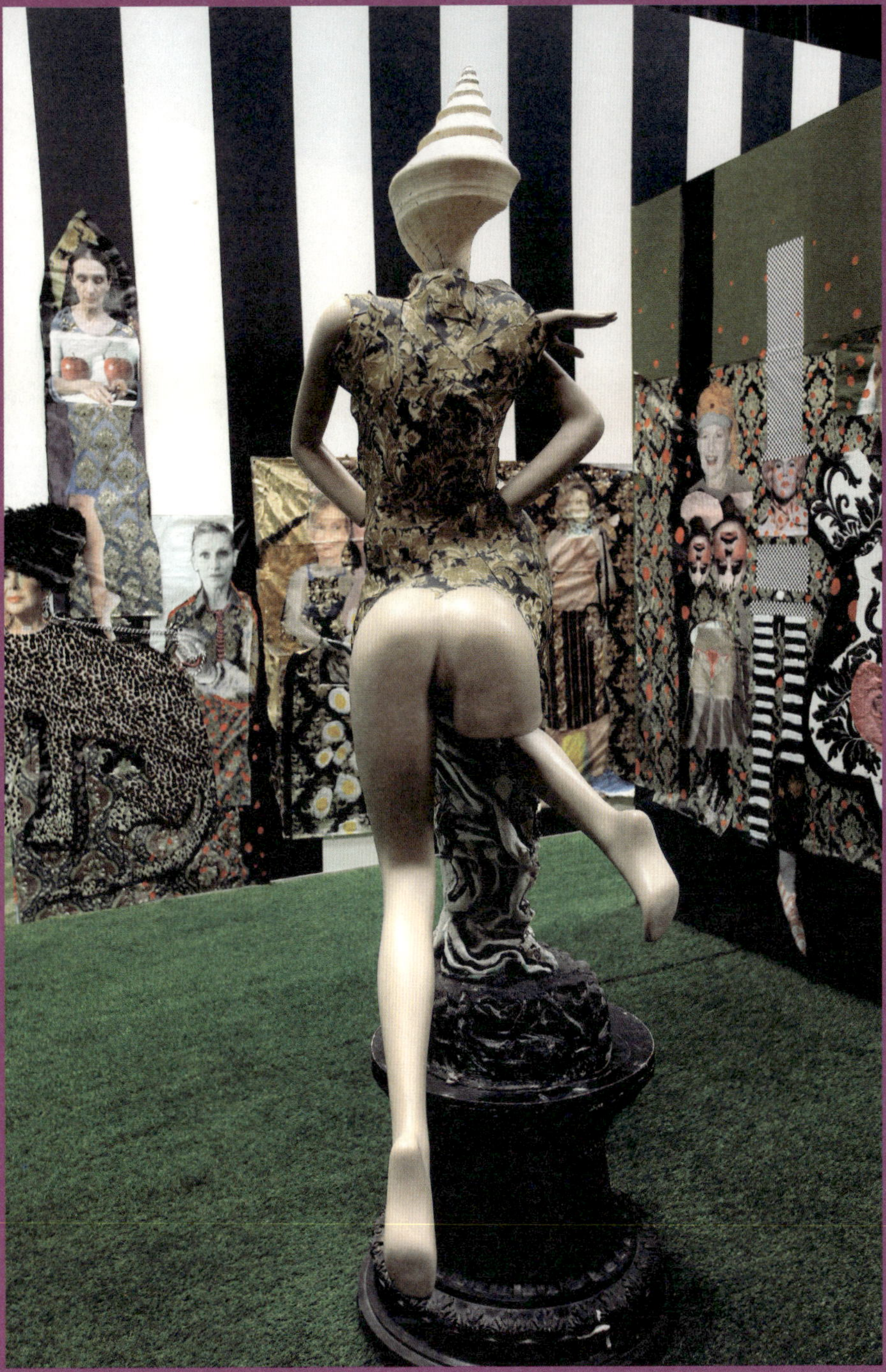

Lady with the Shell, 2012
Fibreglass readymade sculpture, fibreglass mannequin body part,
shell and wallpaper
240 x 109 x 50 cm

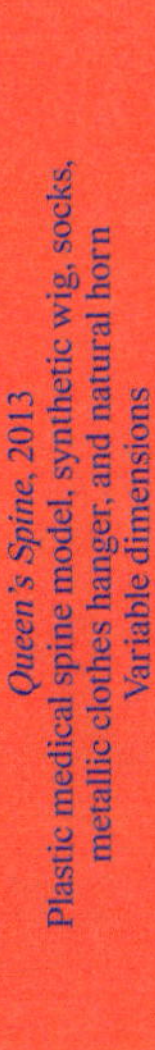

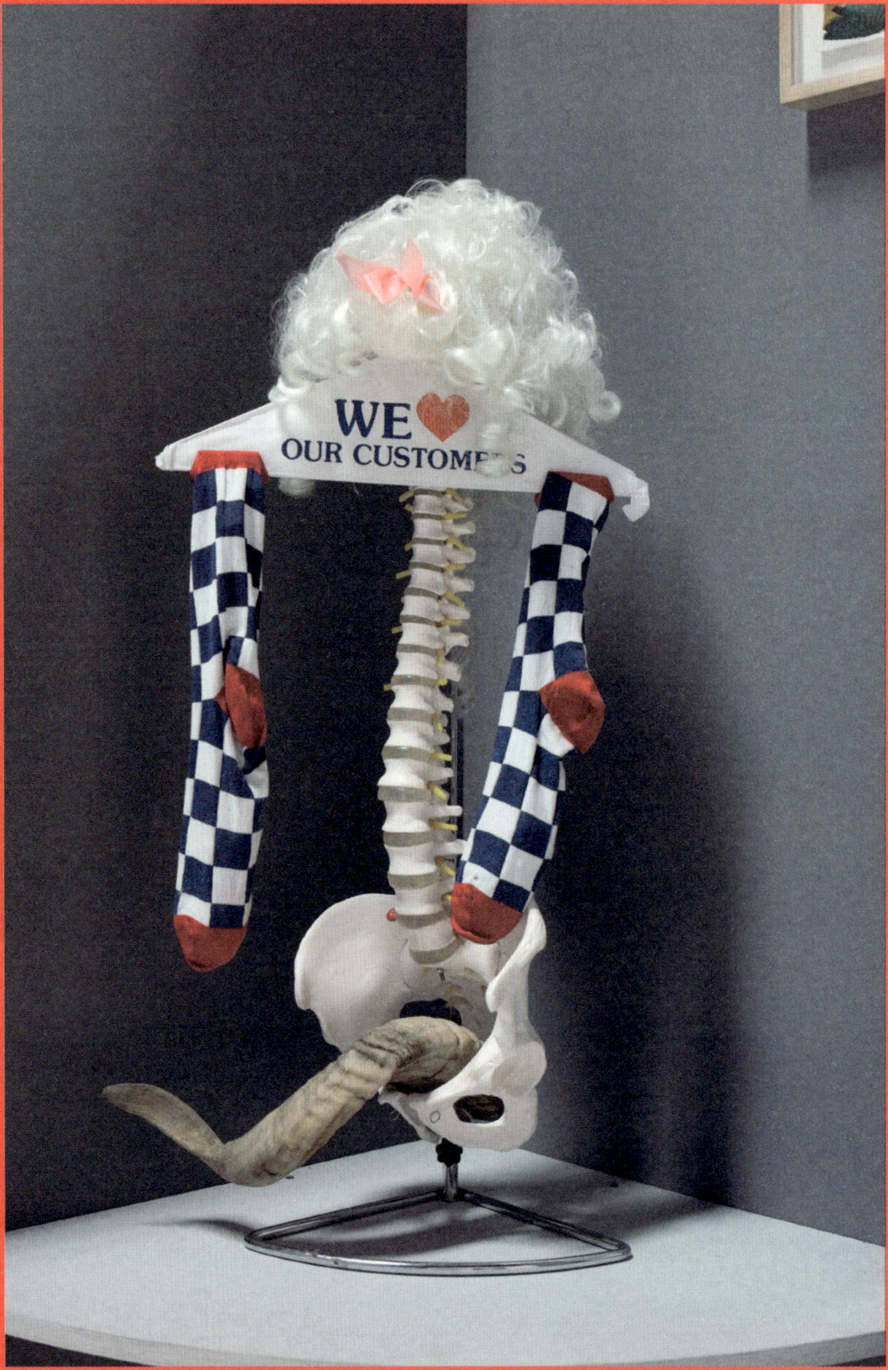

Queen's Spine, 2013
Plastic medical spine model, synthetic wig, socks,
metallic clothes hanger, and natural horn
Variable dimensions

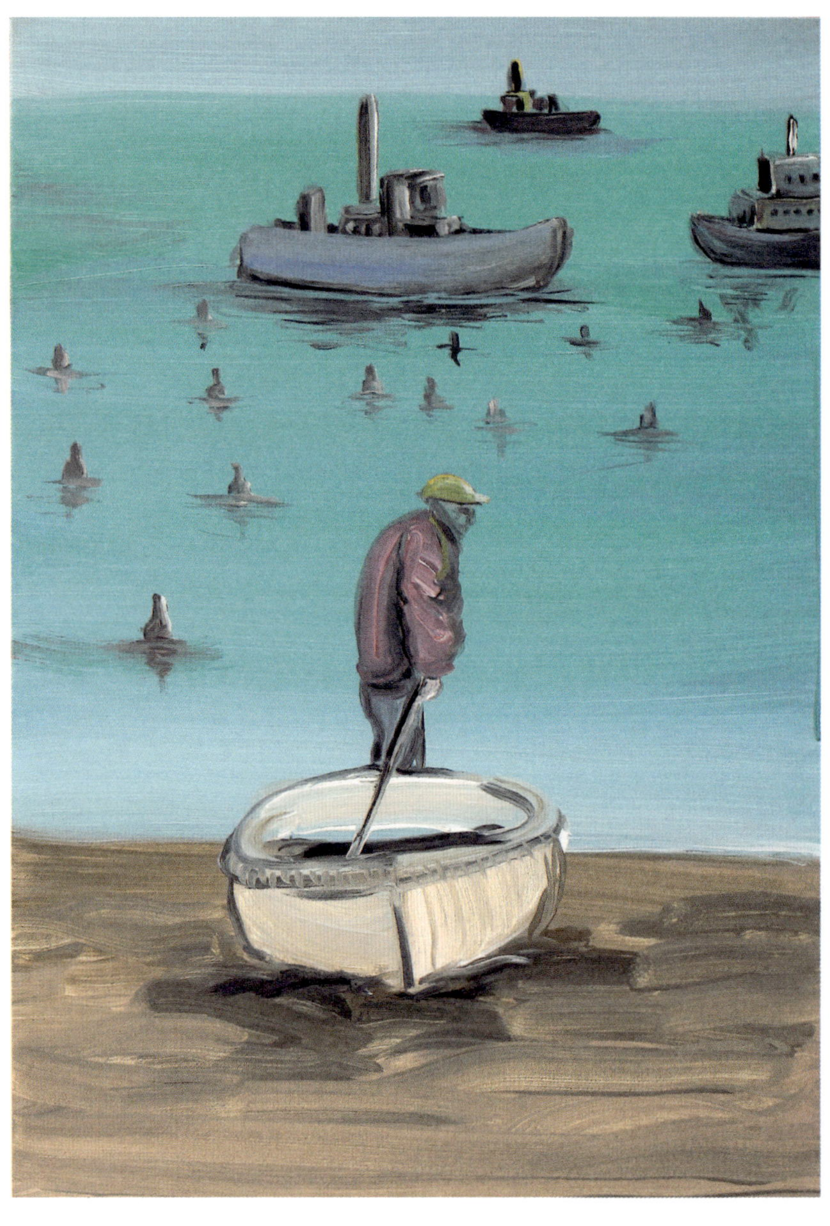

Hesam Rahmanian, Old But Eager, 2012
Acrylic on canvas
70 x 50 cm

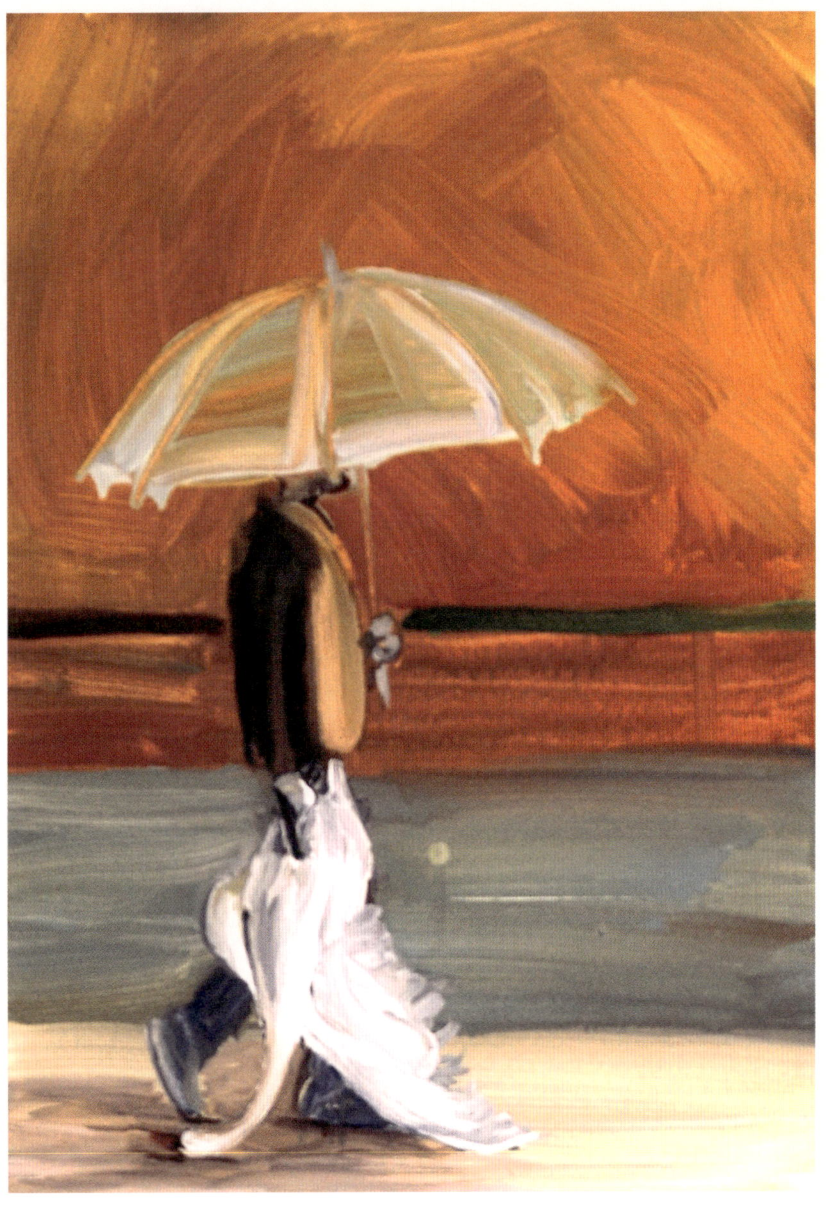

Hesam Rahmanian, *The Savior*, 2012
Acrylic on canvas
70 x 50 cm

47

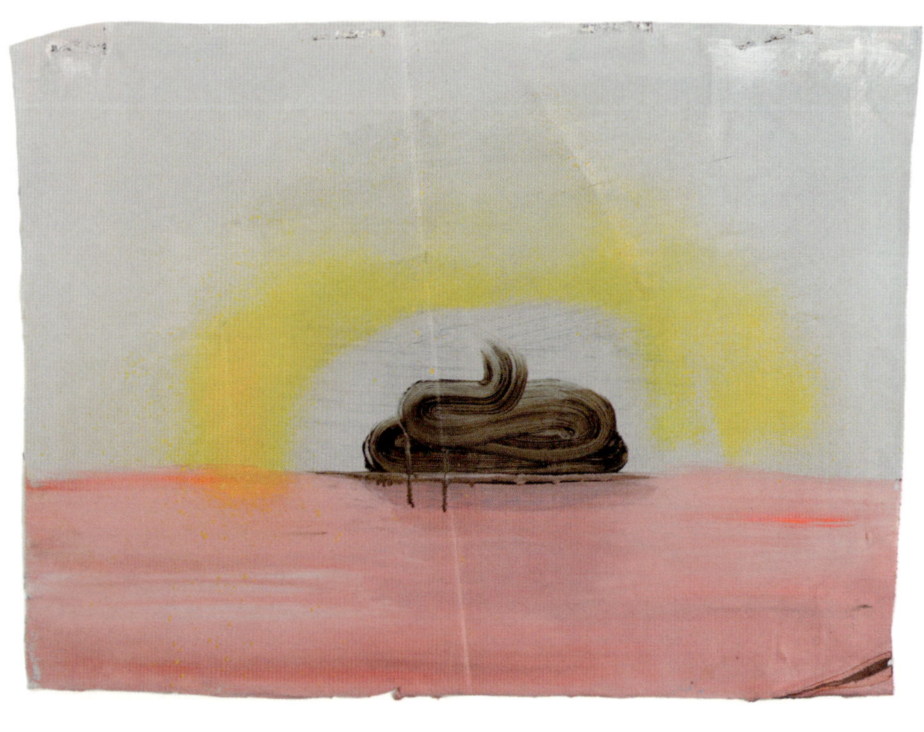

Hesam Rahmanian, *Holy Sh...t!*, 2012
Acrylic and spray paint on canvas
44 x 59 cm

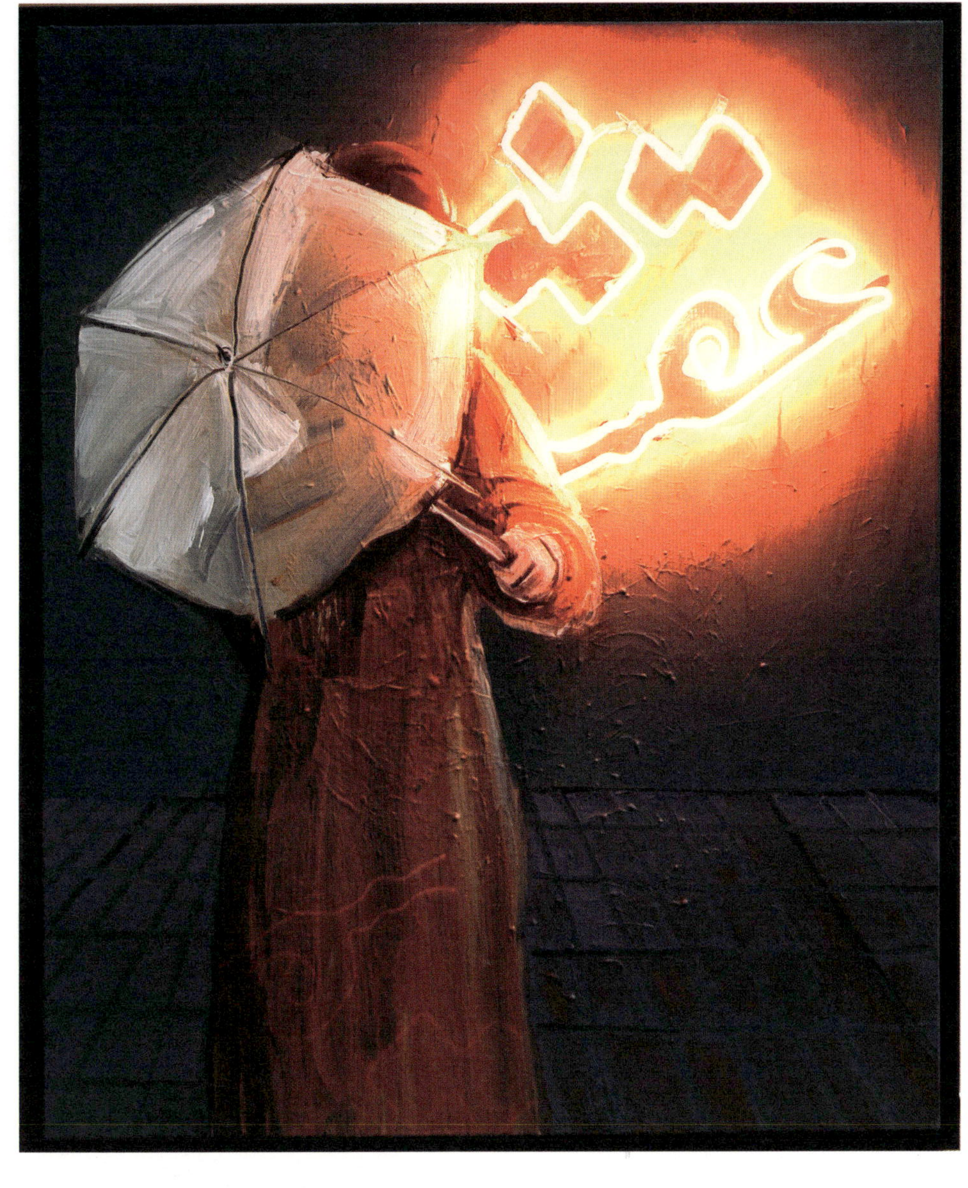

Hesam Rahmanian, *Eqsh (Love)*, 2012
Acrylic and neon on canvas
127 x 107 cm

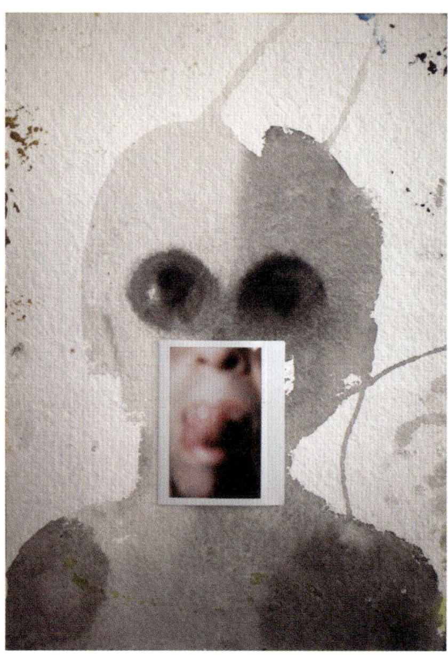

Hesam Rahmanian, *Alien Face*, 2013
Ink and Polaroid photograph on paper
41 x 30 cm

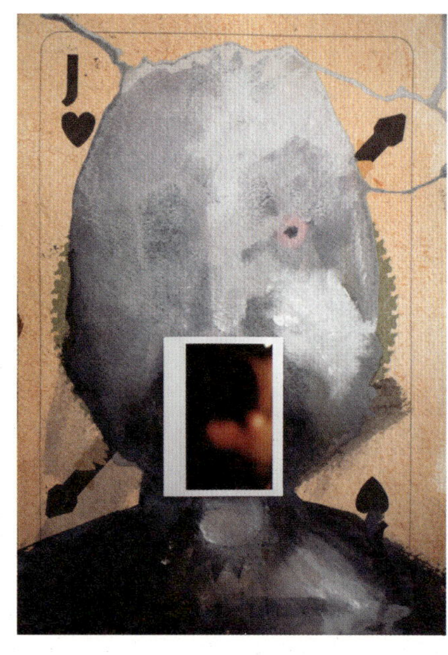

Hesam Rahmanian, *Bearded Dragon Face*, 2013
Ink, acrylic and Polaroid photograph on paper
41 x 30 cm

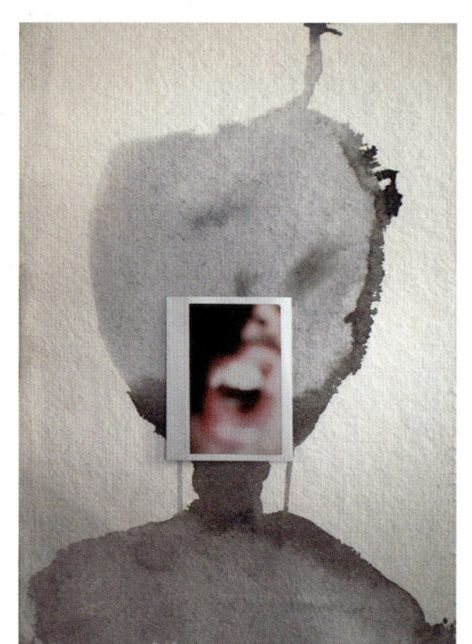

Hesam Rahmanian, *ET Face*, 2013
Ink and Polaroid photograph on paper
41 x 30 cm

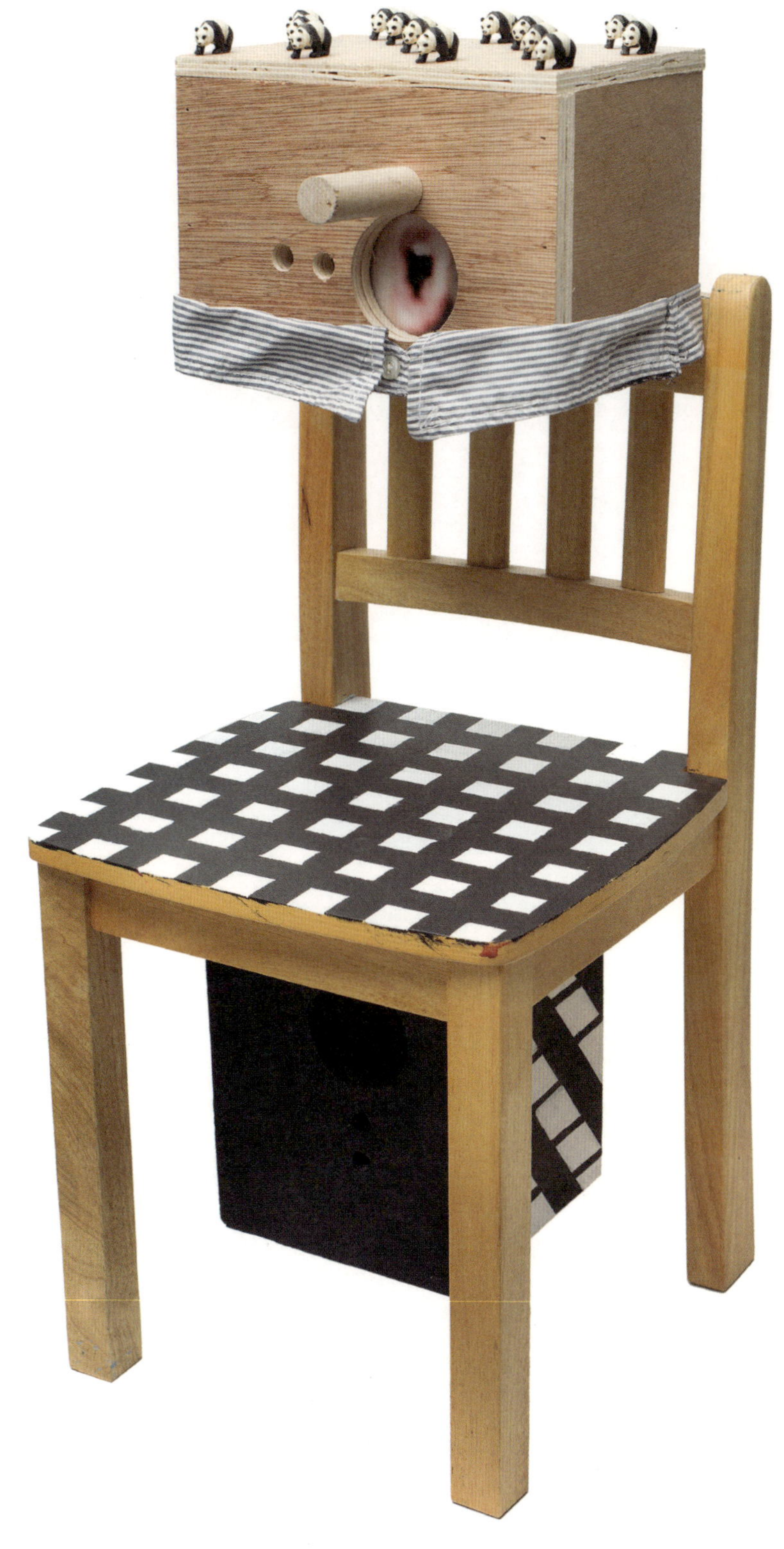

Hesam Rahmanian, *Factory*, 2013
Wooden chair and birdhouses, fabric, plastic panda toys and
Polaroid photograph and acrylic paint
70 x 71 x 30 cm

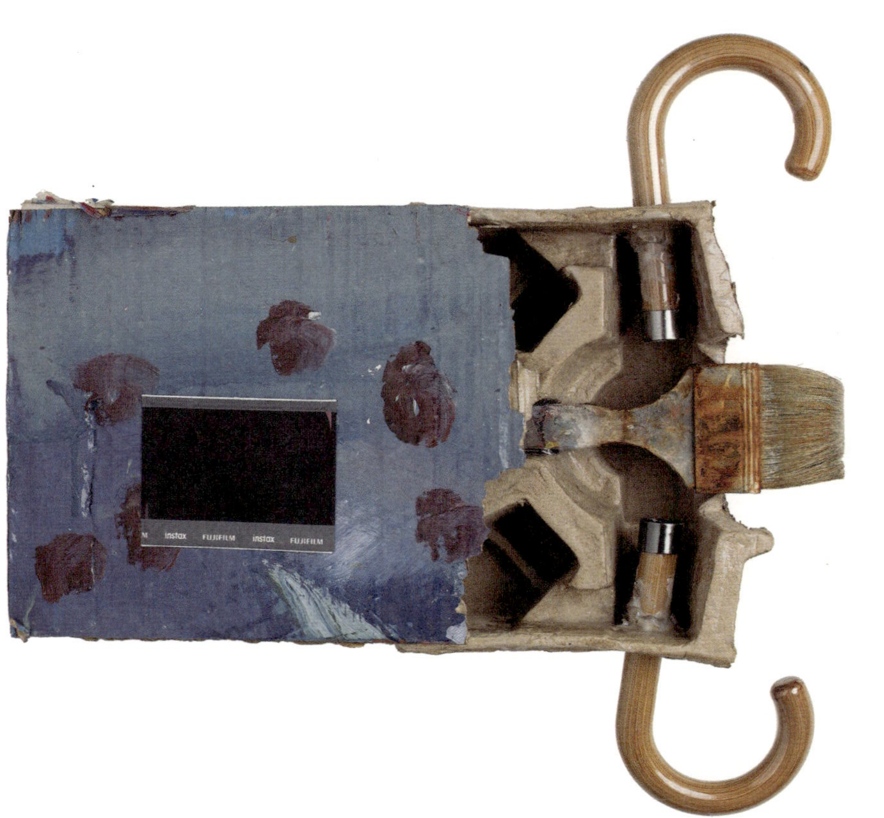

Hesam Rahmanian, *King* (view from back), 2013
Cardboard, wooden paintbrush, acrylic paint, plastic umbrella handles
and Polaroid photographs
45 x 45 x 11 cm

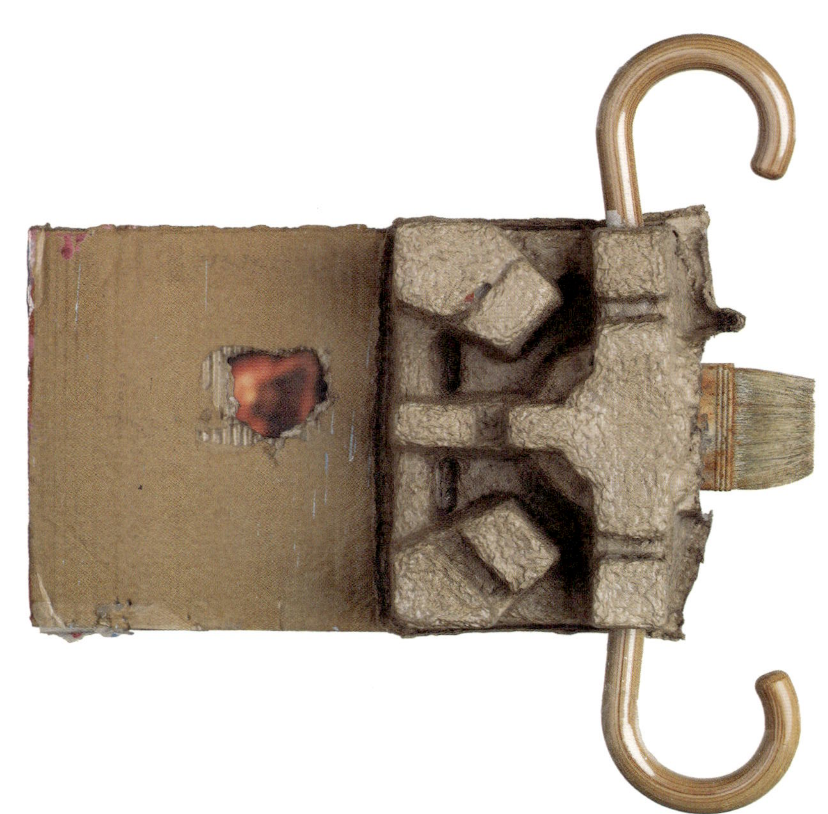

Hesam Rahmanian, *King*, 2013
Cardboard, wooden paintbrush, acrylic paint, plastic umbrella handles
and Polaroid photographs
45 x 45 x 11 cm

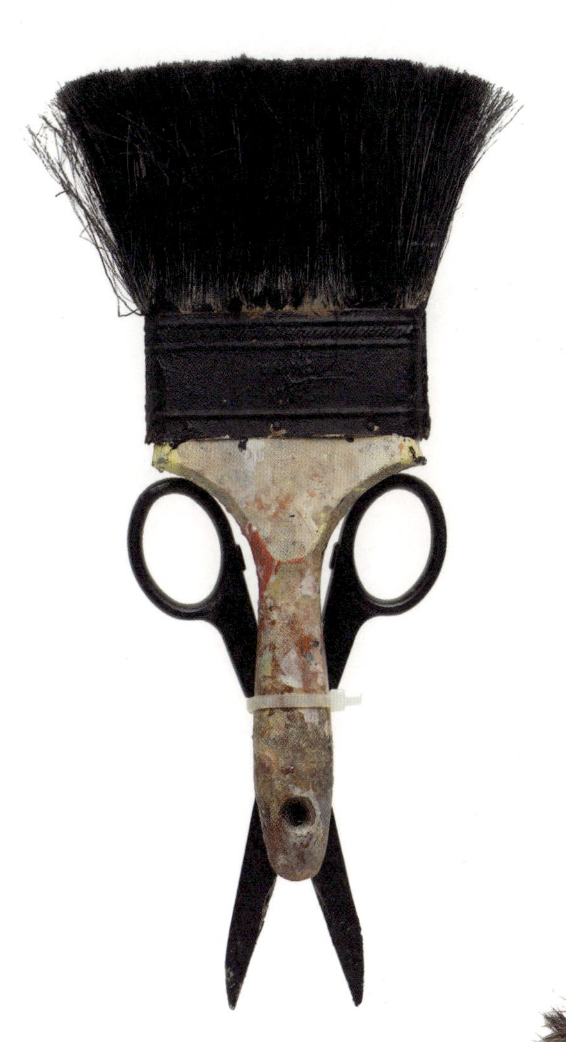

Hesam Rahmanian, *Bird with a Crest*, 2013
Feather duster and scissors
41 x 26 x 20 cm

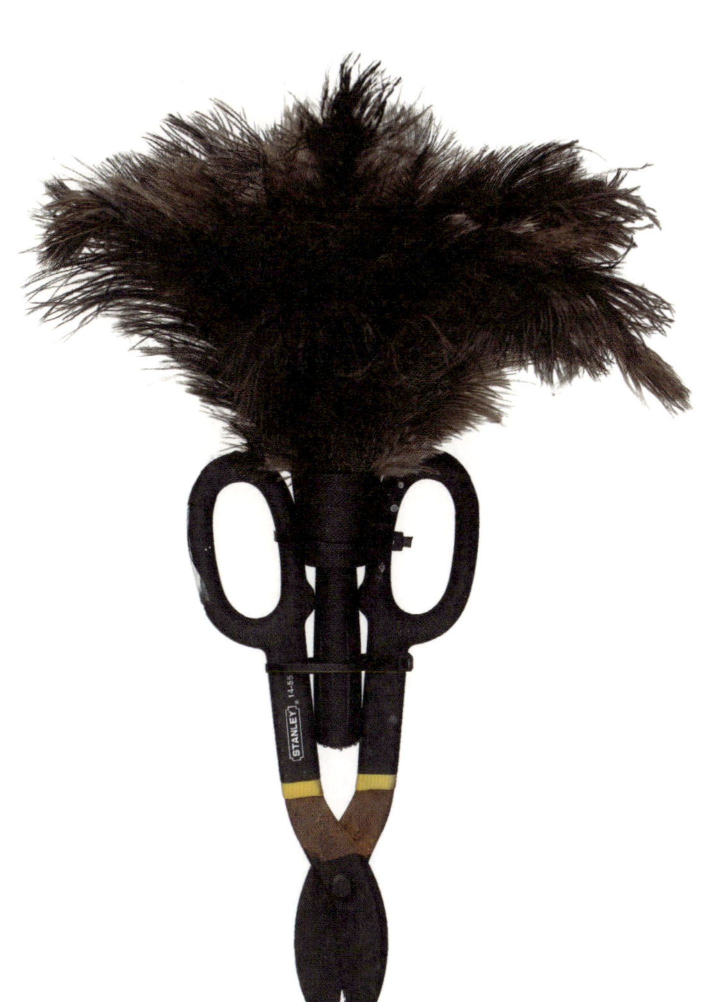

Hesam Rahmanian, *Dude with a Moustache*, 2013
Wooden paintbrush and scissors
33 x 17 x 4 cm

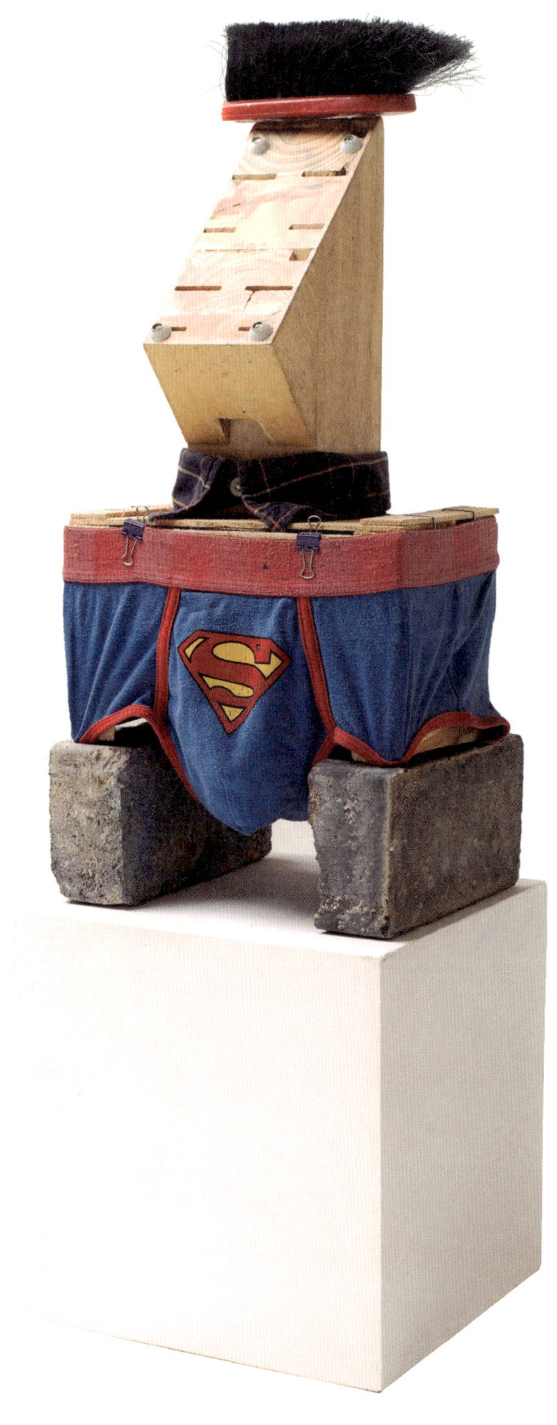

Hesam Rahmanian, *Superman*, 2013
Underwear, dustpan brush, wooden fruit basket, wooden knife holder
and two concrete blocks
80 x 26.5 x 26.5 cm

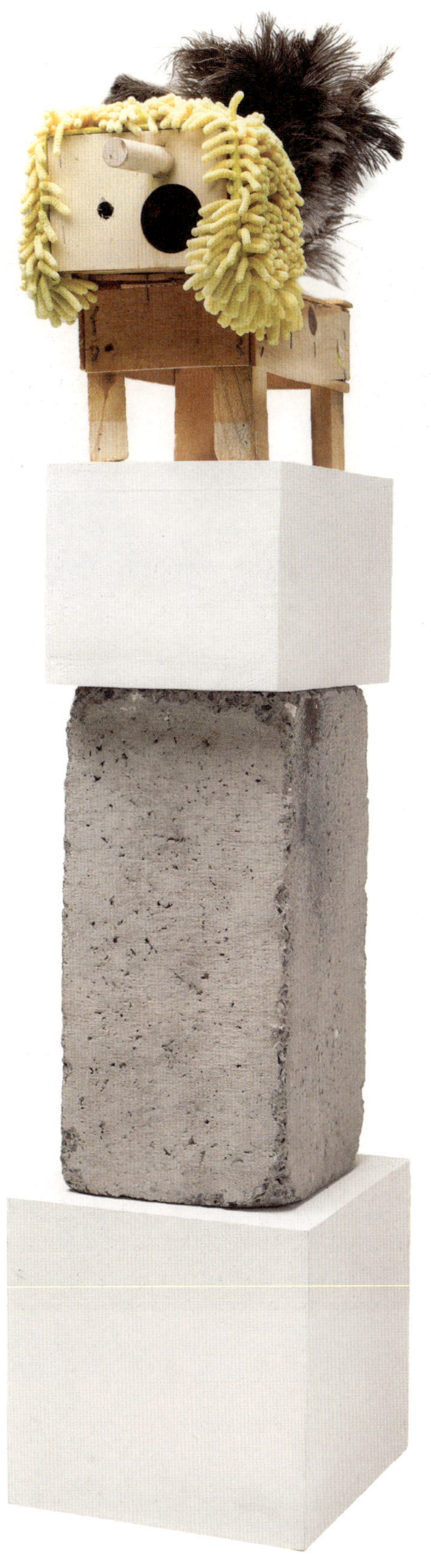

Hesam Rahmanian, *Lion*, 2013
Feather duster, cotton mop, wooden fruit basket, wooden birdhouse,
wooden boxes and concrete block
70 x 31 x 30 cm

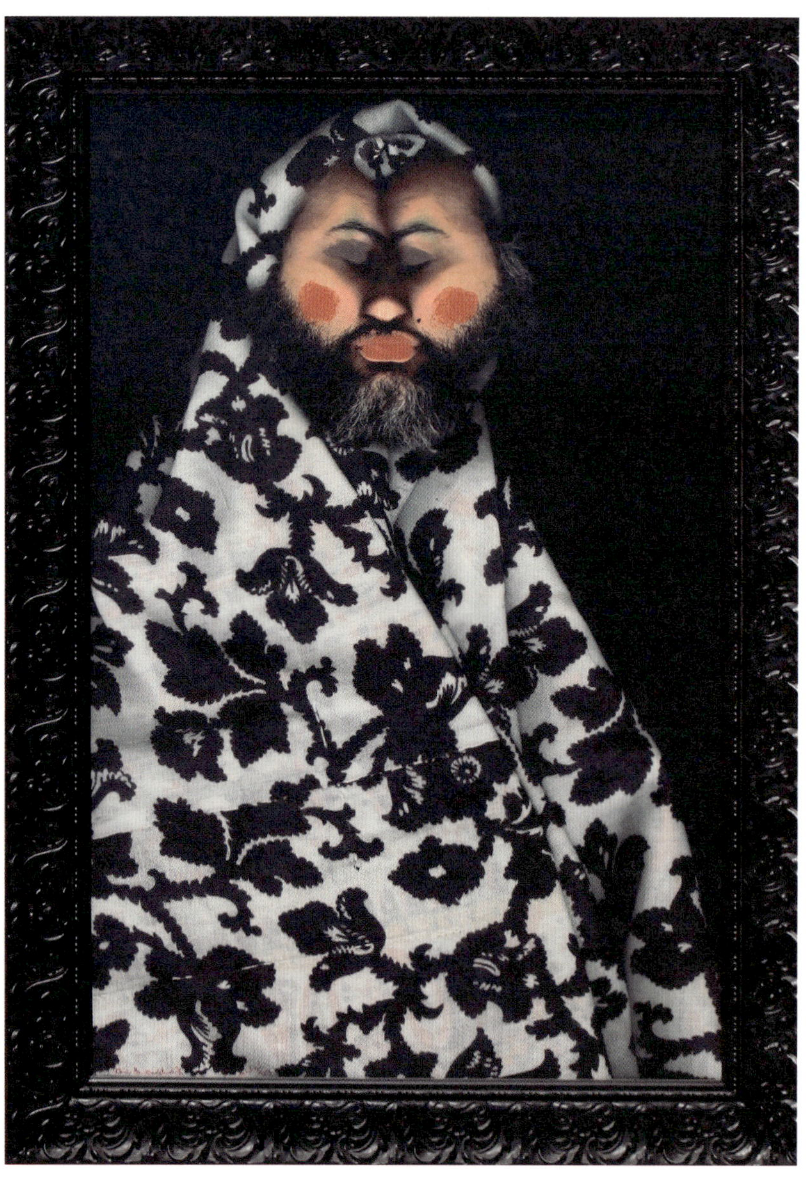

Ramin Haerizadeh, *Theatre Group*, 2008
Lambda print
100 x 70 cm

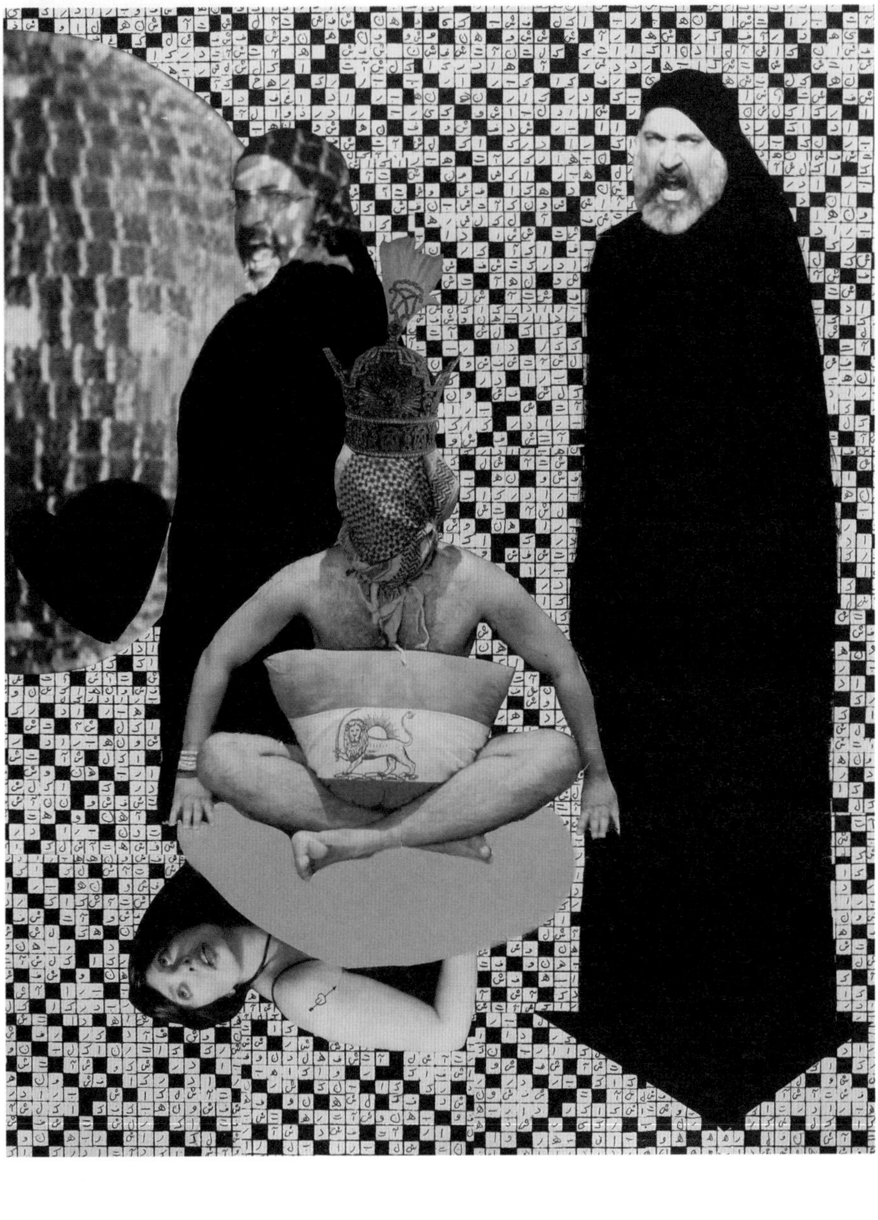

Ramin Haerizadeh, *We Choose to Go to the Moon*, 2009
Collage and acrylic on canvas
200 x 150 cm

Ramin Haerizadeh, *Rib Room*, 2013
Paper collage, ink and pencil on paper
35.5 x 25.5 cm

Ramin Haerizadeh, *Still Life, King and Queen Tomato*, 2011
Paper collage, acrylic and ink on canvas
170 x 140 cm

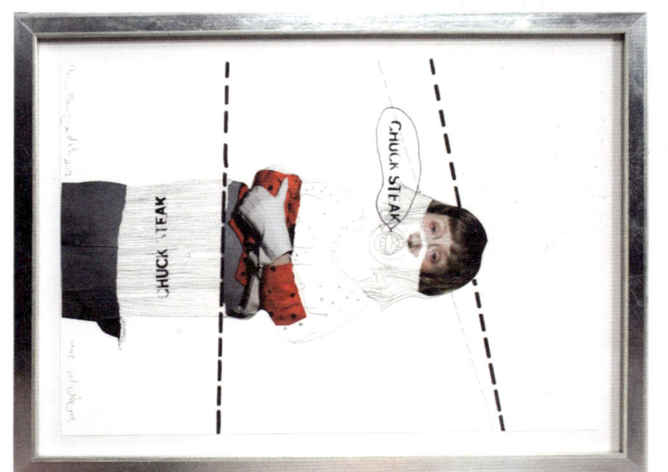
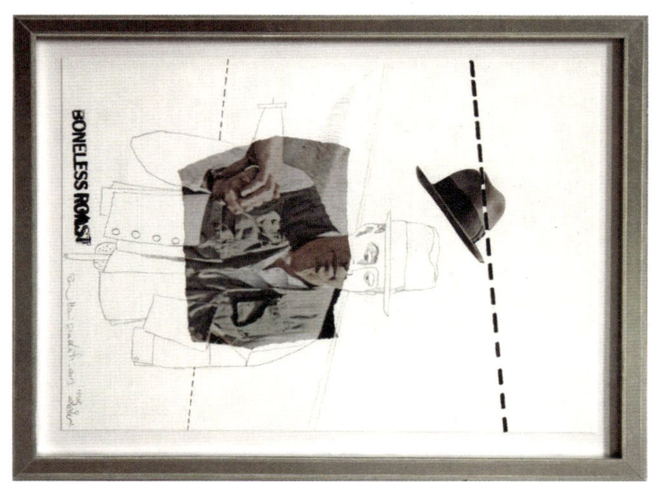

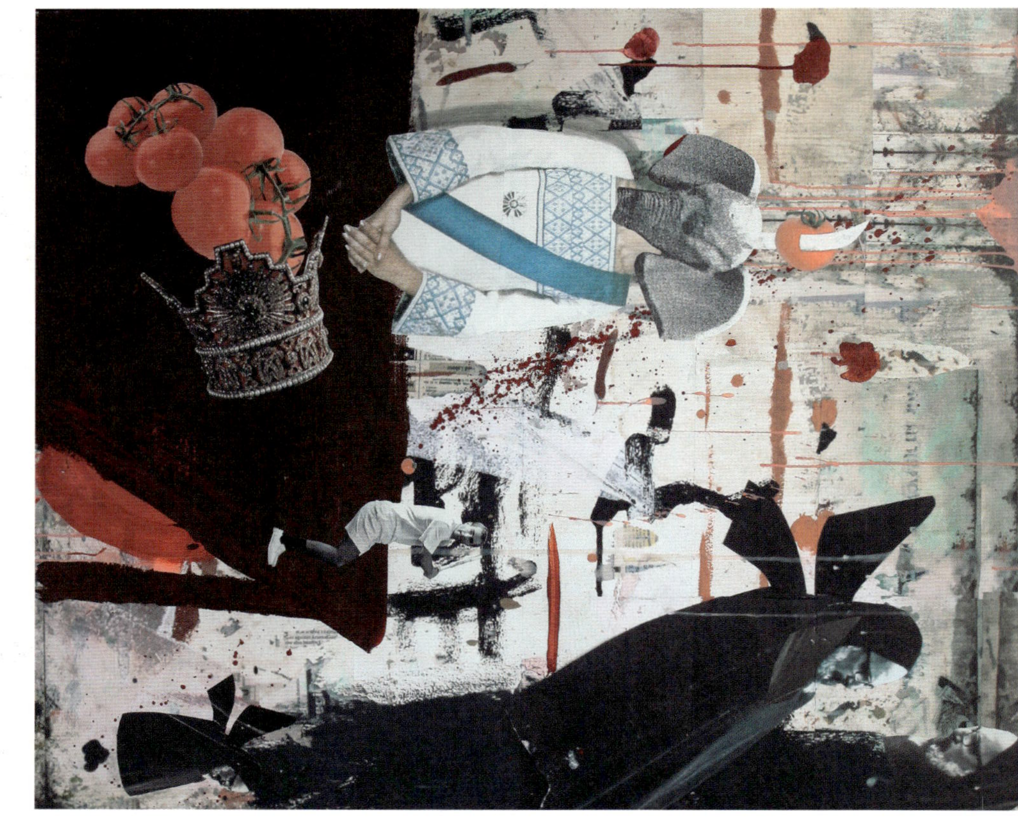

Ramin Haerizadeh, *Emperor's New Dress*, 2014
Paper collage and spray paint on canvas, ornamented gilded frames sticks,
rattan blind, wooden table, synthetic hair, water pump motor, plastic pipes, goat skull,
terracotta sculpture, plastic nose, plastic ribbons and fake chicken leg
250 x 160 x 100 cm

Ramin Haerizadeh, *Emperor's New Dress* (detail), 2014
Paper collage and spray paint on canvas, ornamented gilded frames sticks,
rattan blind, wooden table, synthetic hair, water pump motor, plastic pipes, goat skull,
terracotta sculpture, plastic nose, plastic ribbons and fake chicken leg
250 x 160 x 100 cm

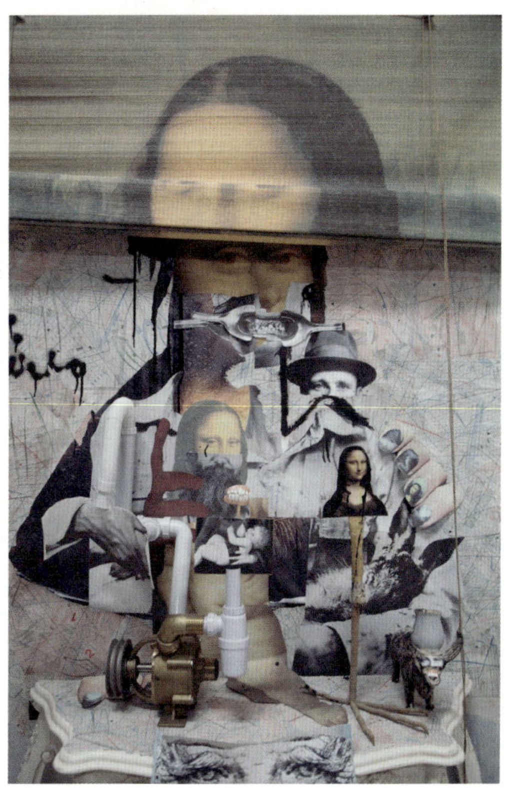

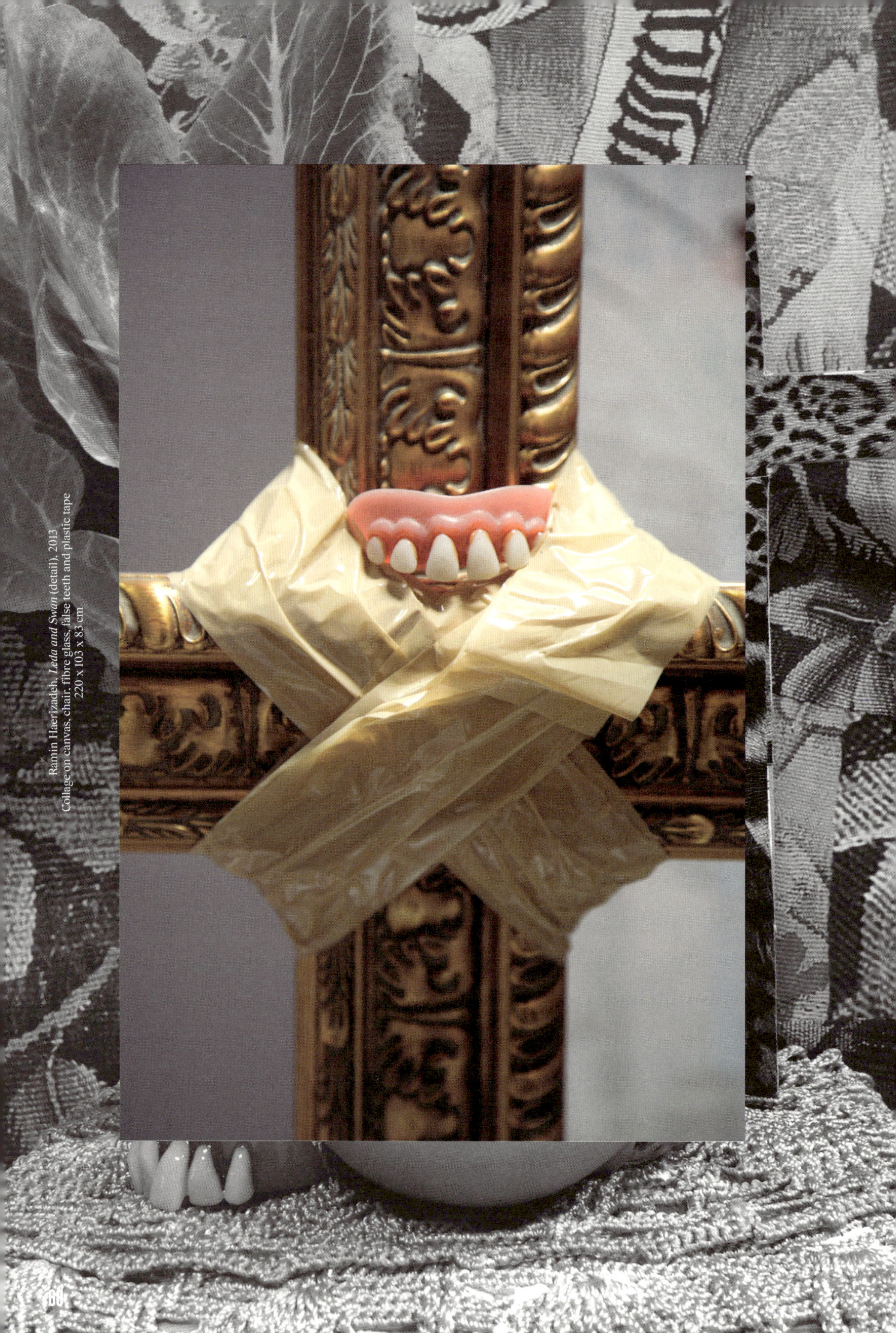

Ramin Haerizadeh, *Leda and Swan* (detail), 2013
Collage on canvas, chair, fibre glass, false teeth and plastic tape
220 x 103 x 83 cm

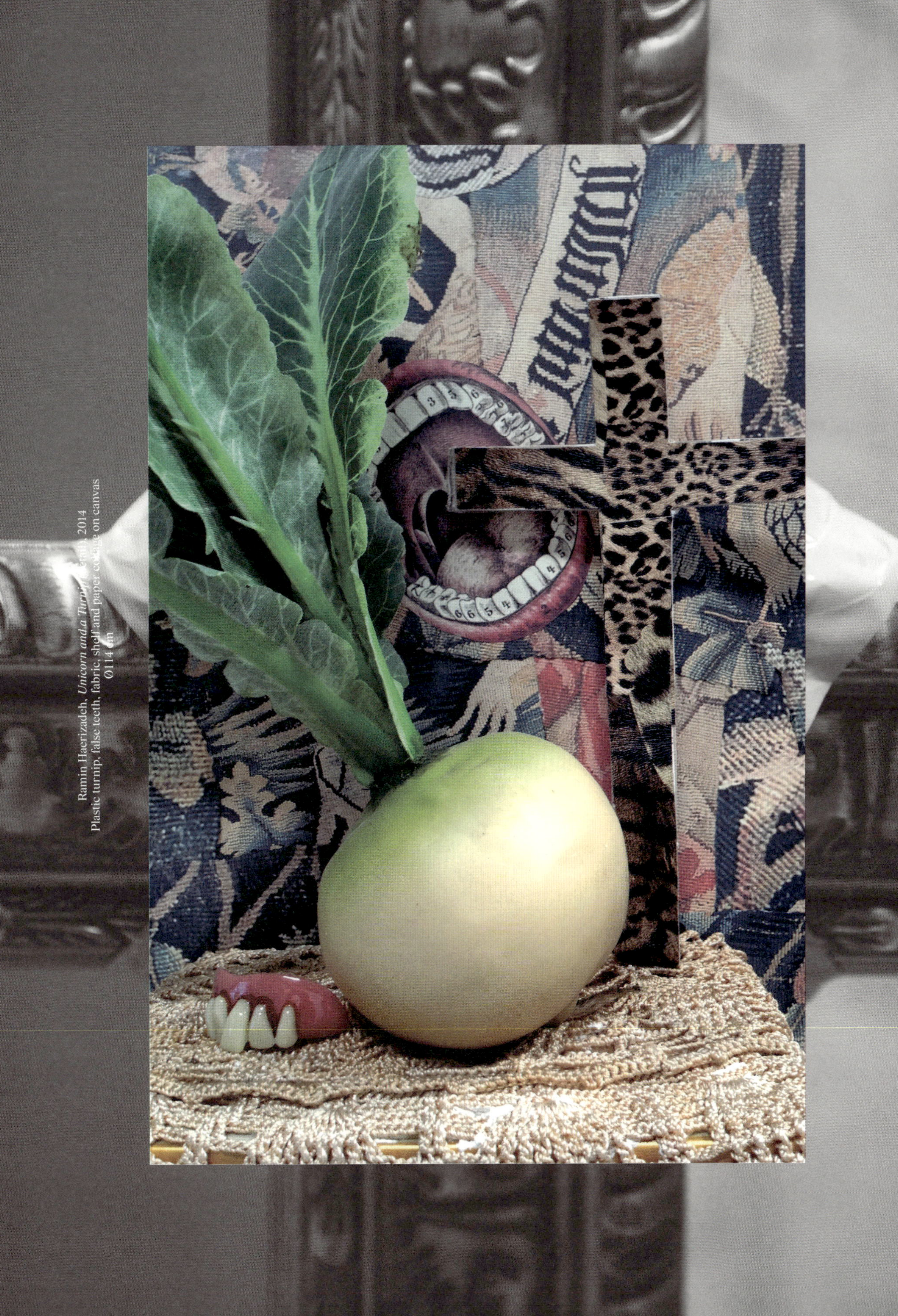

Ramin Haerizadeh, *Unicorn and a Turnip* (teeth), 2014
Plastic turnip, false teeth, fabric, shelf and paper collage on canvas
Ø114 cm

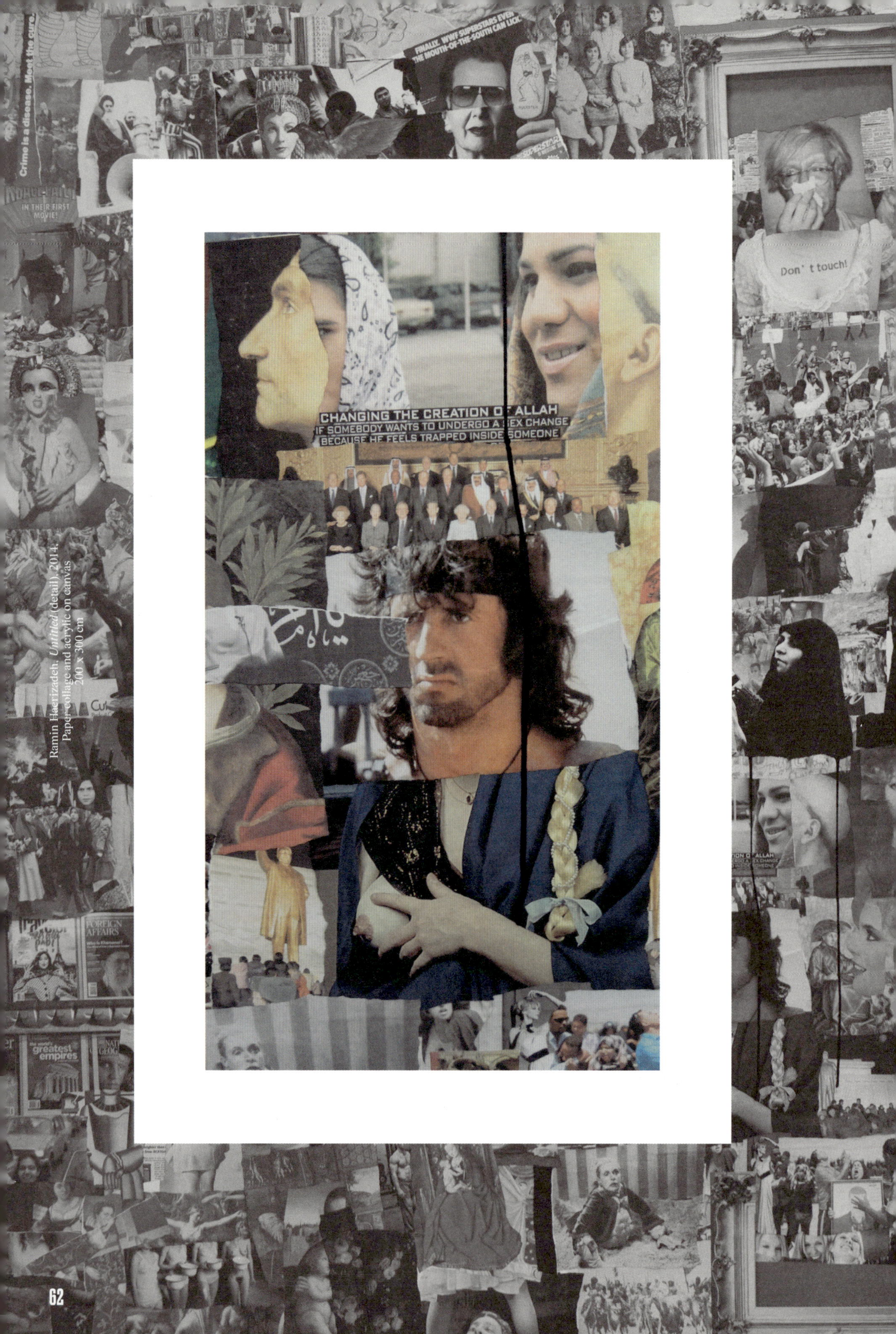

Ramin Haerizadeh. *Untitled* (detail). 2014.
Paper collage and acrylic on canvas
200 x 300 cm

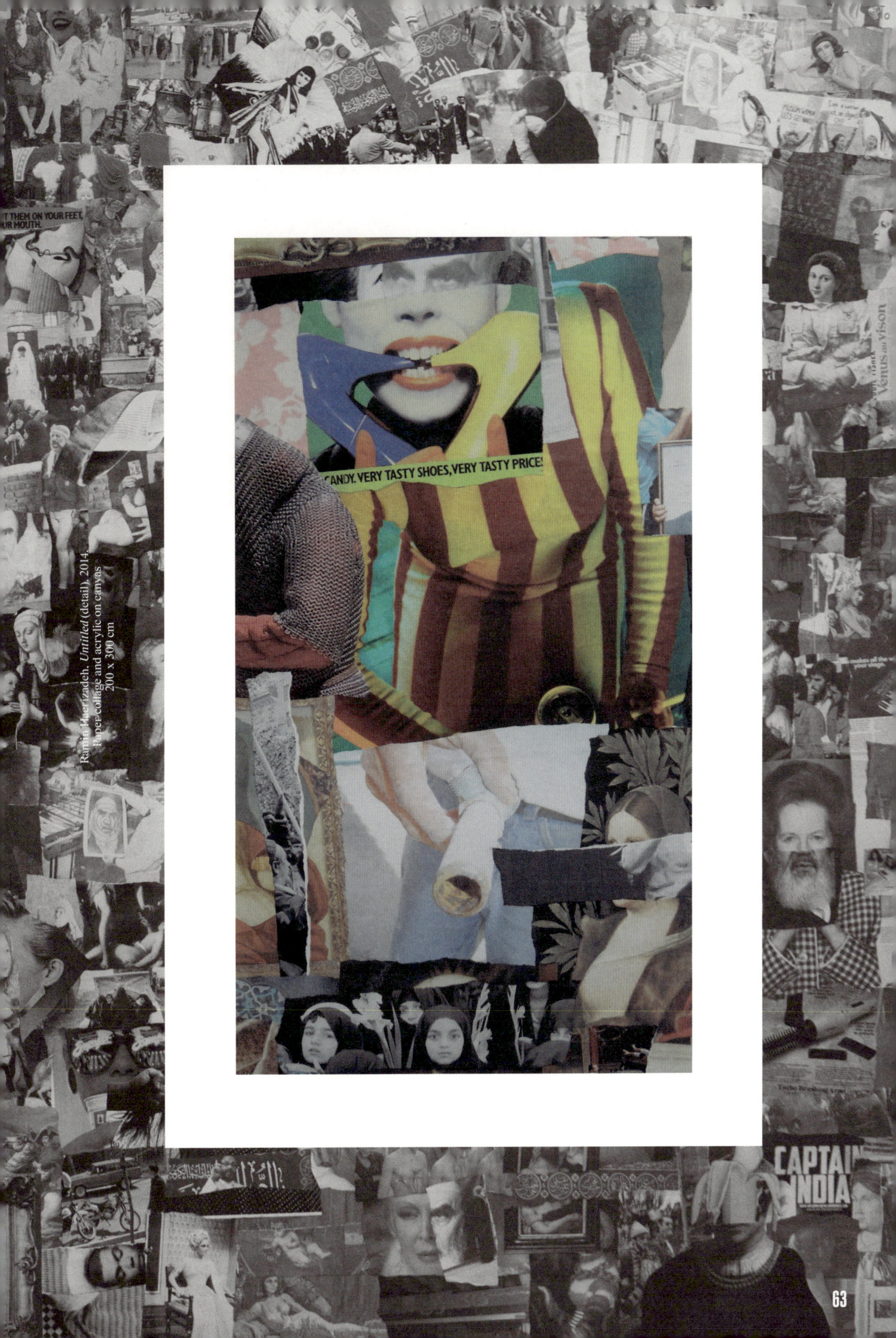

Ramin Haerizadeh. *Untitled* (detail), 2014.
Paper collage and acrylic on canvas
200 x 300 cm

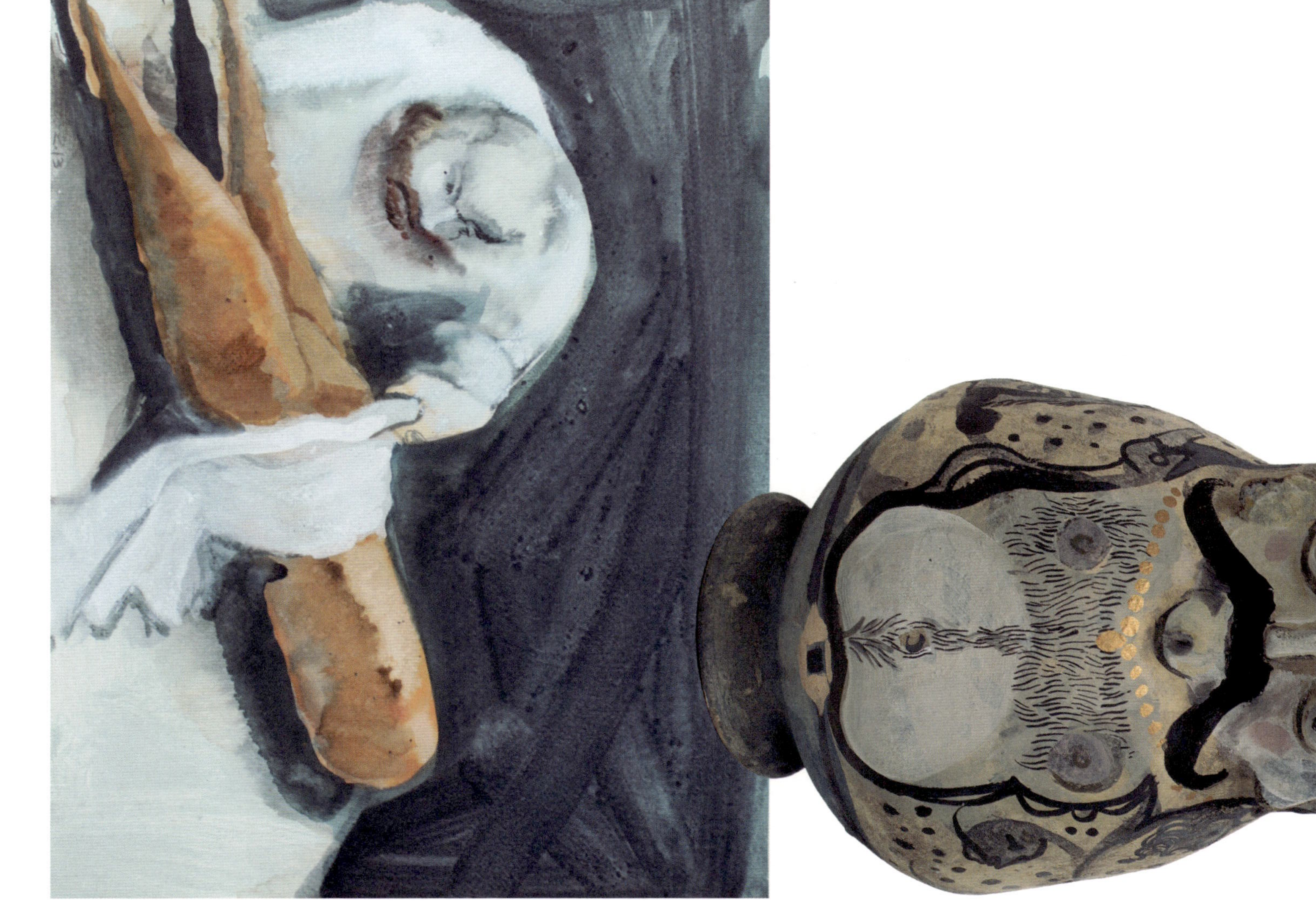

Rokni Haerizadeh, *A Carrot and Randy*, 2013
Watercolour and ink on paper
30 x 40 cm

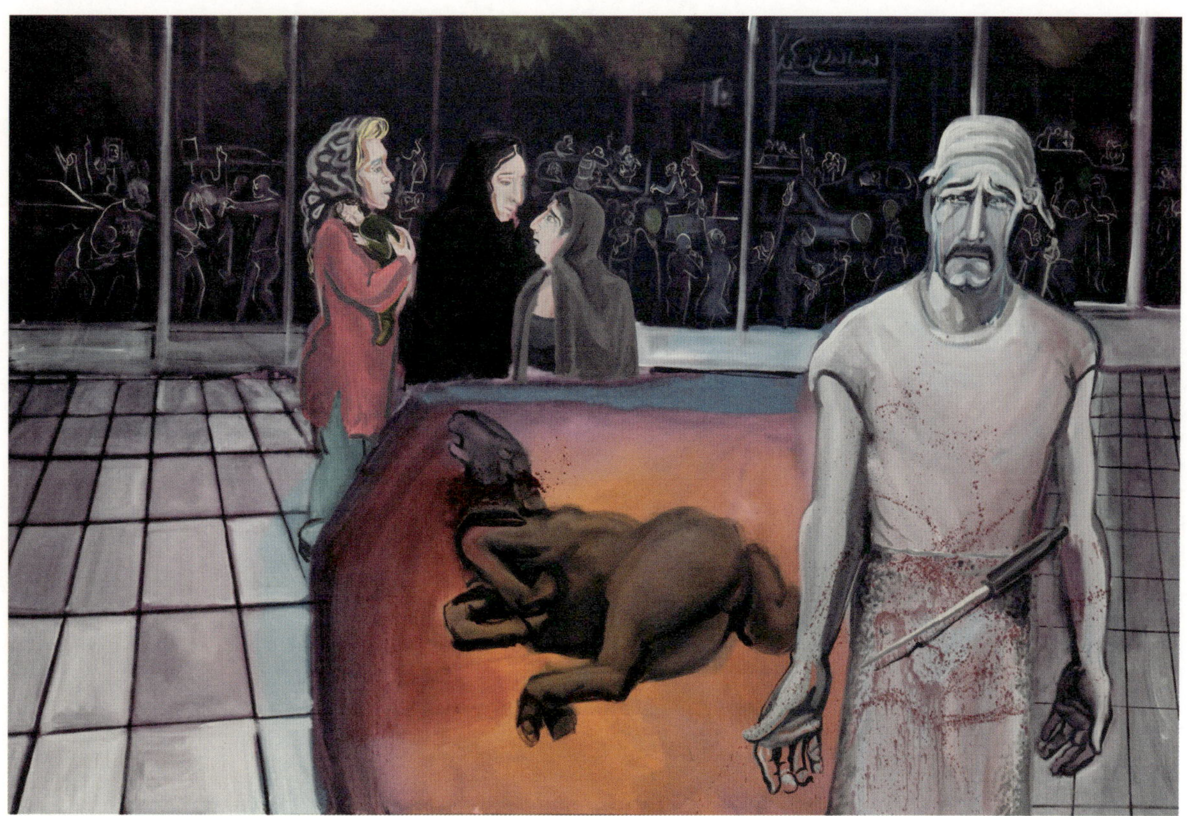

Rokni Haerizadeh, *The Crying Butcher Was in Love with the Canary*, 2009
Oil on canvas
200 x 300 cm

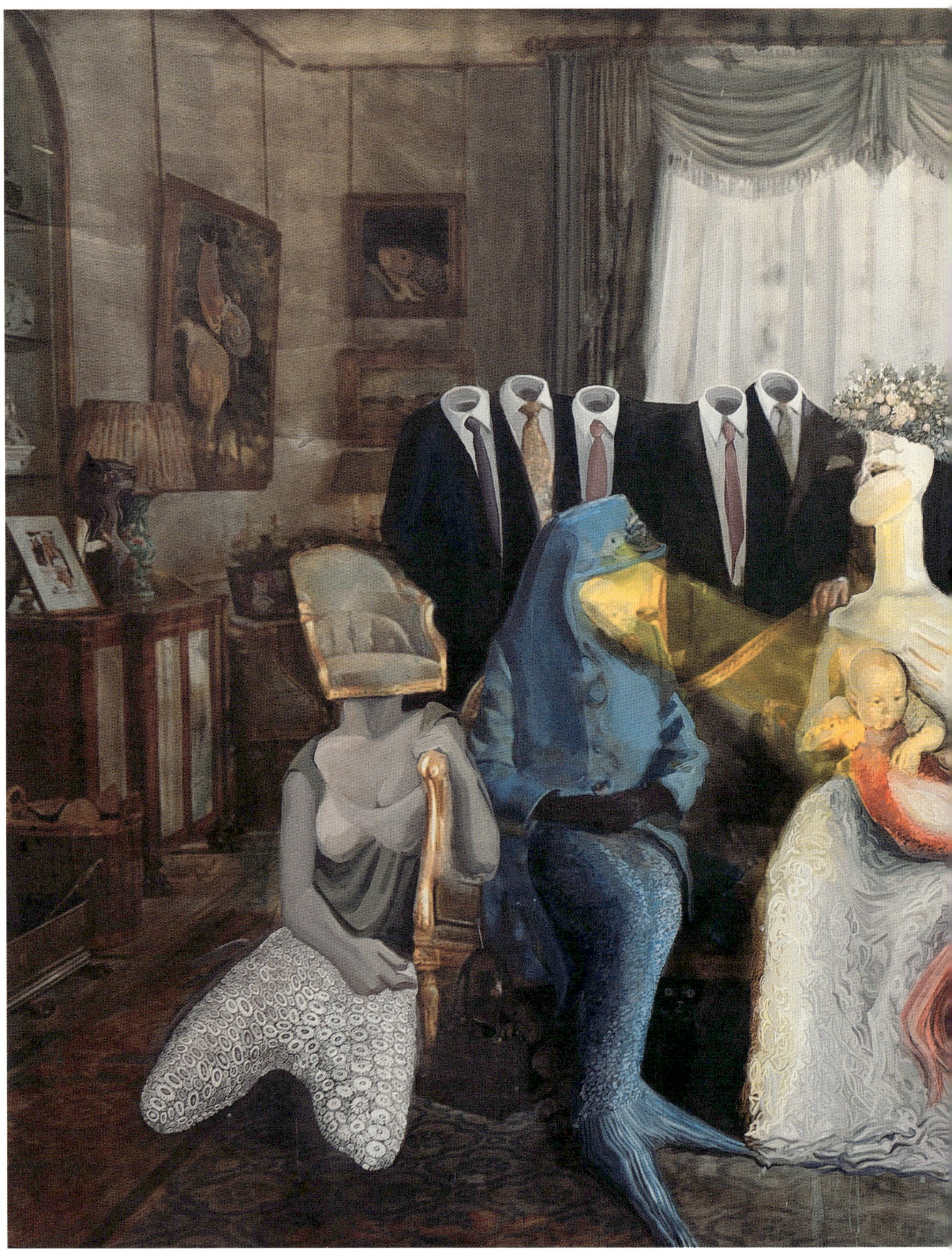

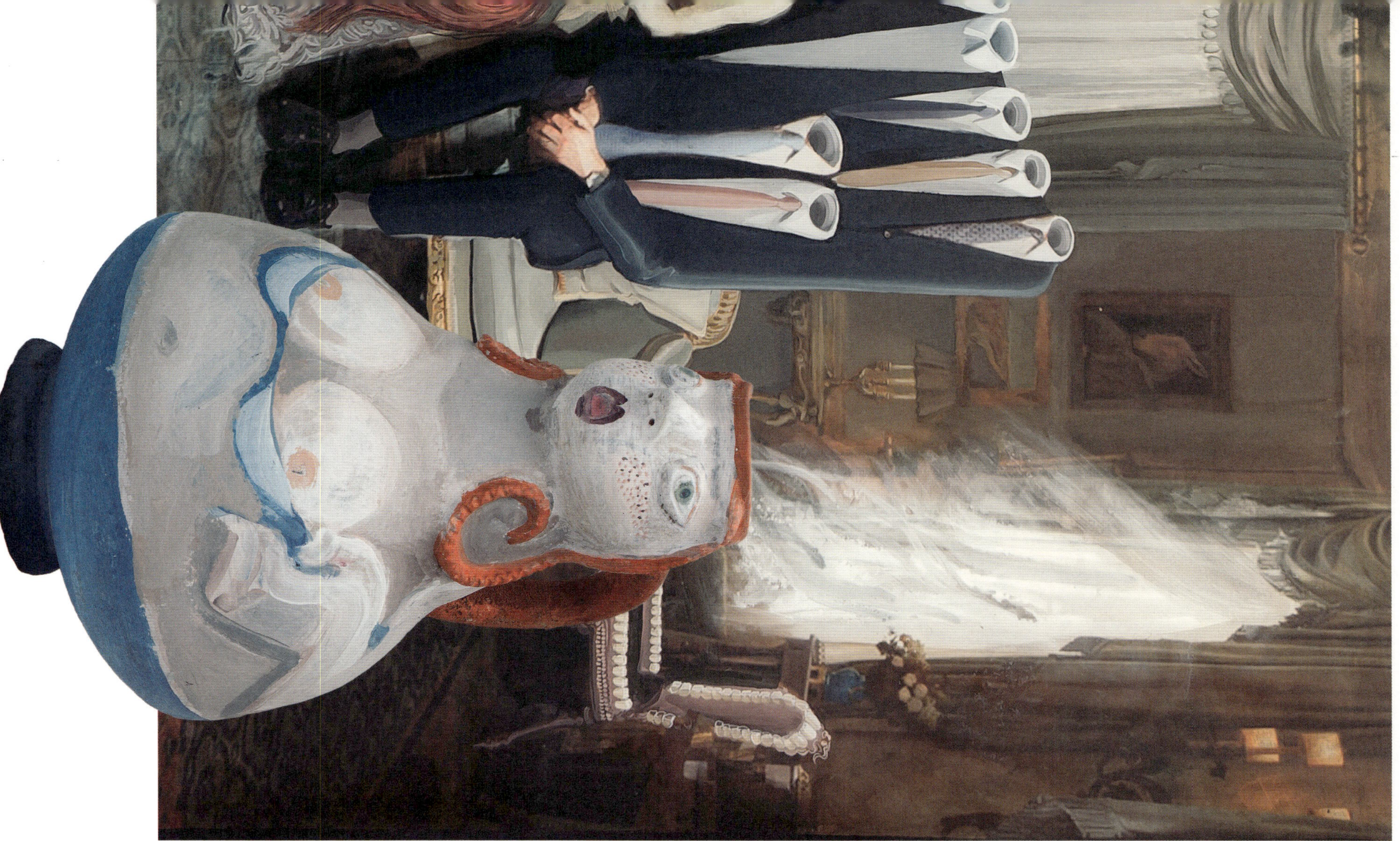

Rokni Haerizadeh, *Royal Goldfish*, 2014
Gesso, acrylic, watercolour and ink on canvas
300 x 435 cm

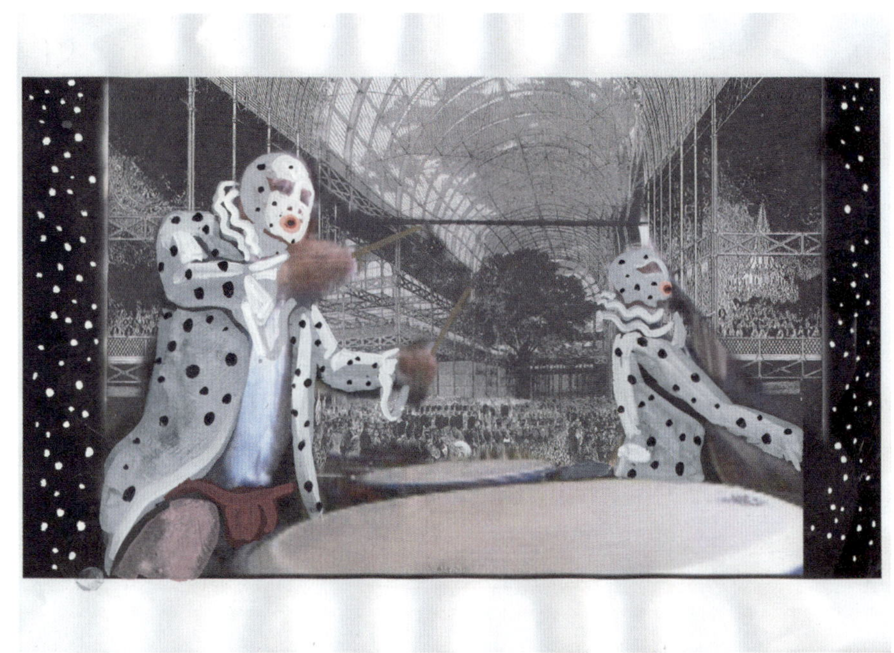

Rokni Haerizadeh, *Reign of Winter*, 2012 – 2013
Single channel colour video (rotoscoping)
Still from the animation, 8' 42''

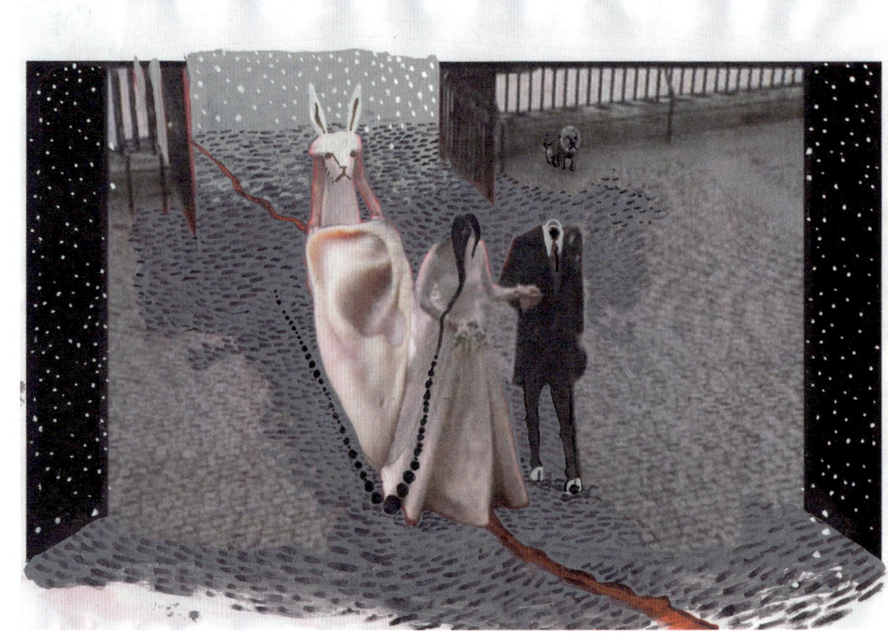

Rokni Haerizadeh, *Reign of Winter*, 2012 – 2013
Single channel colour video (rotoscoping)
Still from the animation, 8' 42''

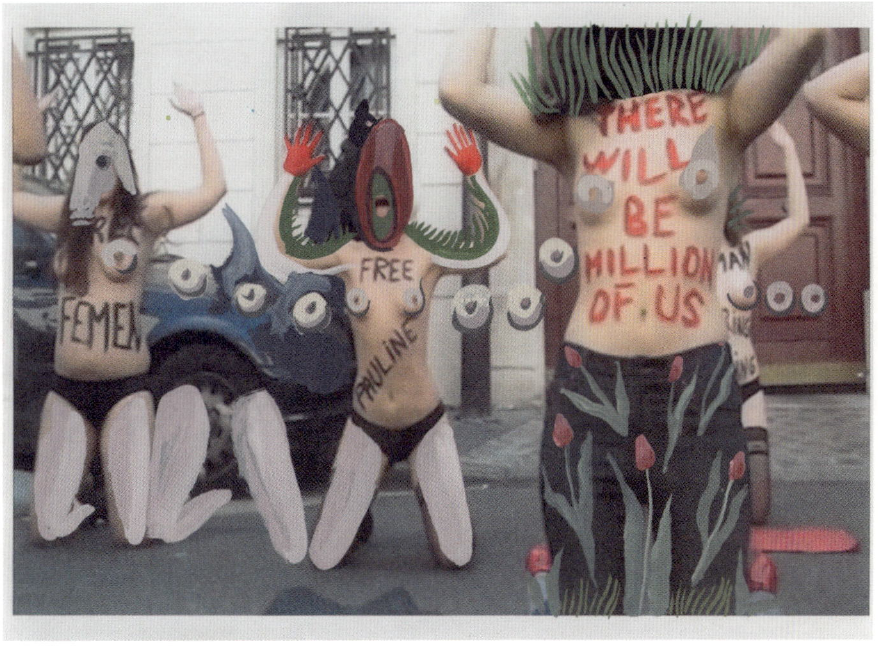

Rokni Haerizadeh, *Letter!*, 2014
Single channel colour video (rotoscoping)
Still from the animation, 6'32"

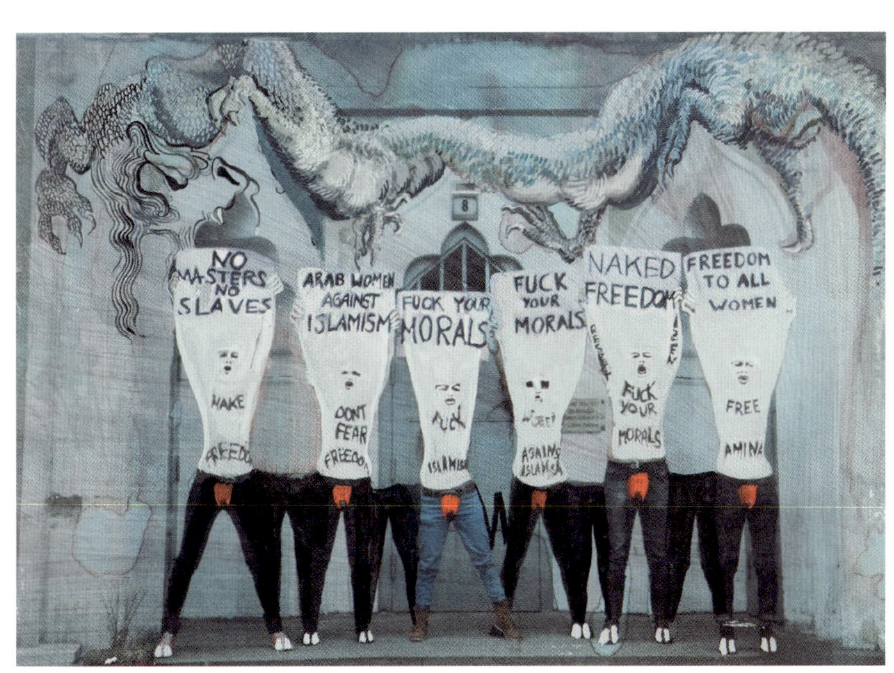

Rokni Haerizadeh, *Subversive Salami in a Ragged Briefcase*, 2014
Gesso, watercolour and ink on printed paper
30 x 40 cm

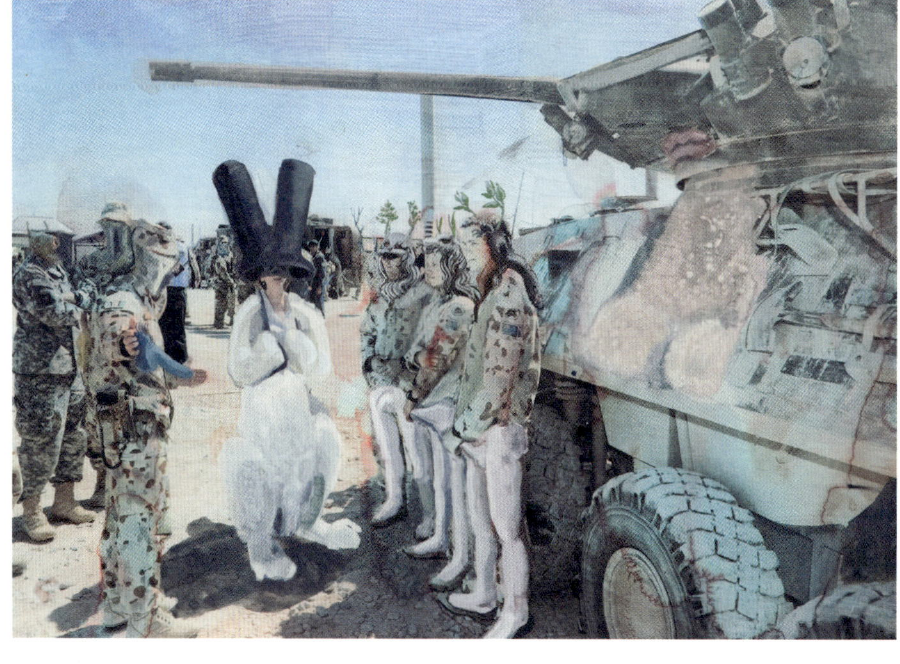

Rokni Haerizadeh, *Subversive Salami in a Ragged Briefcase*, 2014
Gesso, watercolour and ink on printed paper
30 x 40 cm

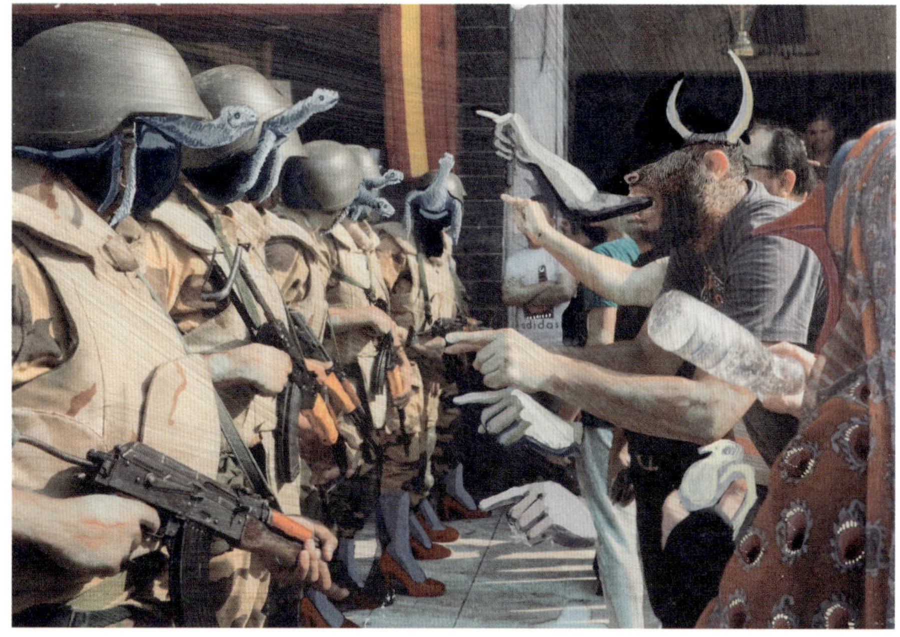

Rokni Haerizadeh, *Subversive Salami in a Ragged Briefcase*, 2014
Gesso, watercolour and ink on printed paper
30 x 40 cm

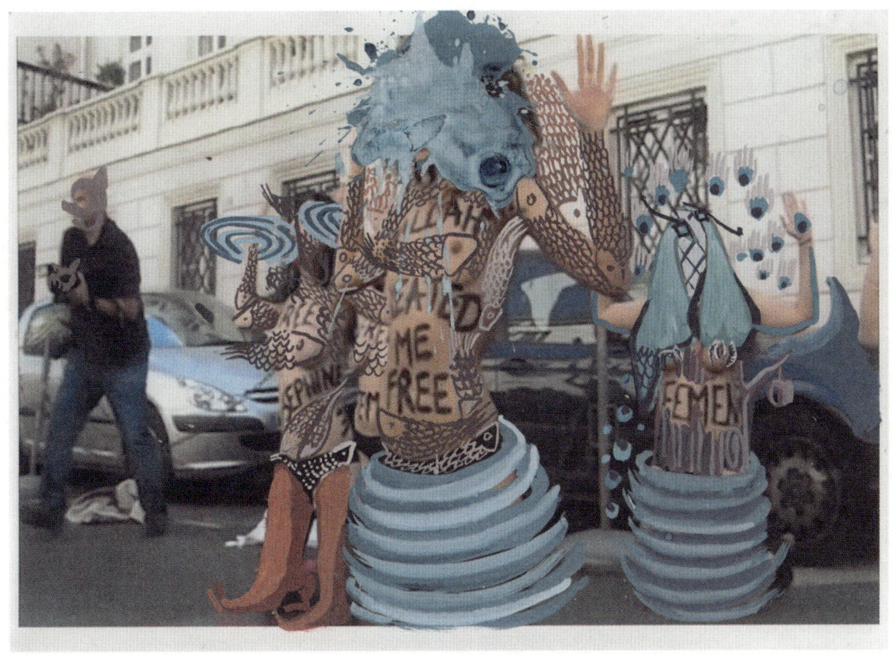

Rokni Haerizadeh, *Letter!*, 2014
Single channel colour video (rotoscoping)
Still from the animation, 6'32''

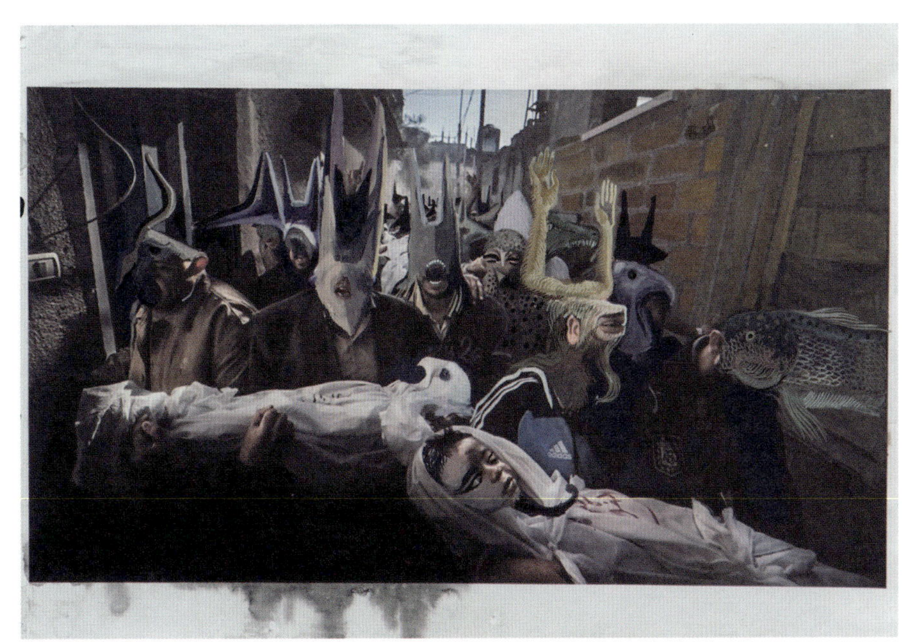

Rokni Haerizadeh, *Subversive Salami in a Ragged Briefcase*, 2014
Gesso, watercolour and ink on printed paper
30 x 40 cm

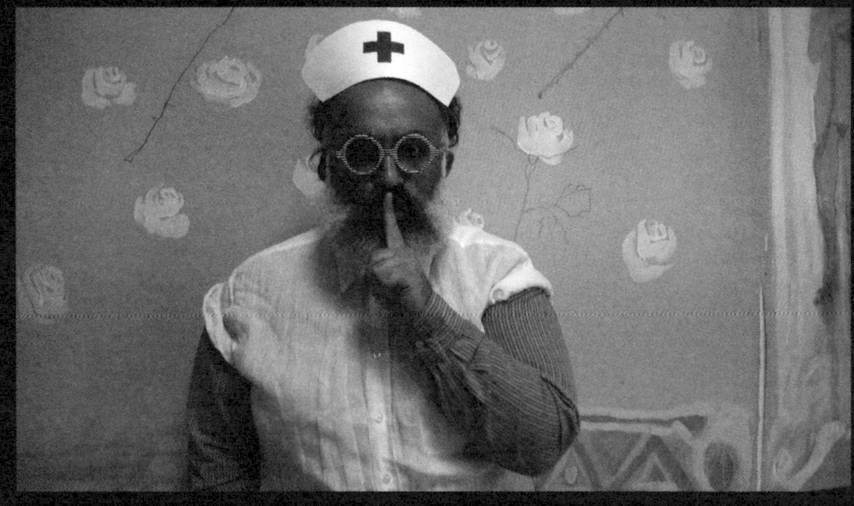

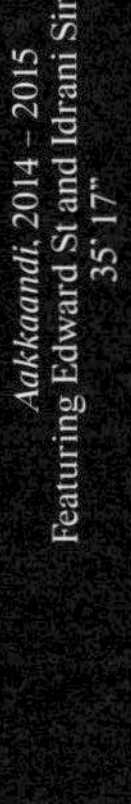
Aakkaandi, 2014 – 2015
Featuring Edward St and Idrani Sirisena
35' 17"

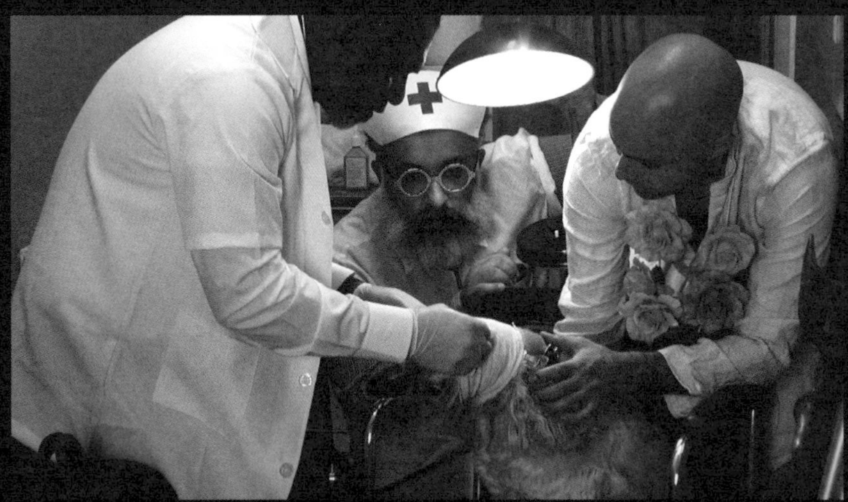

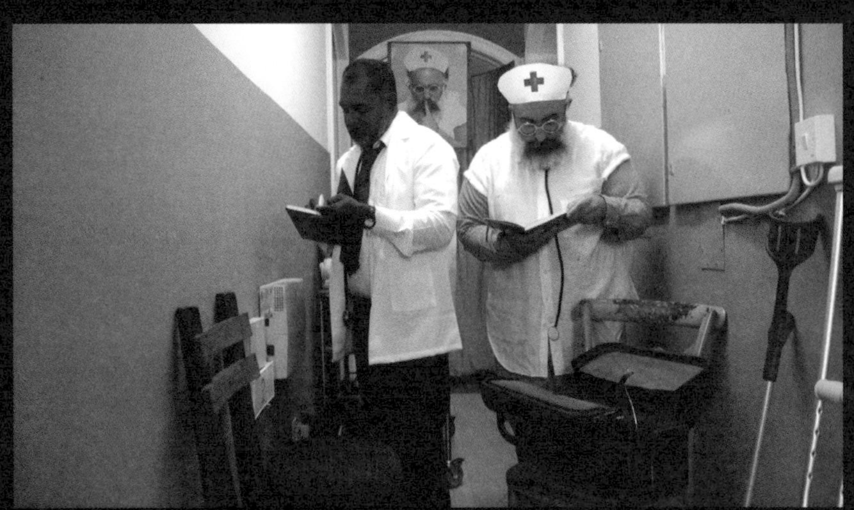

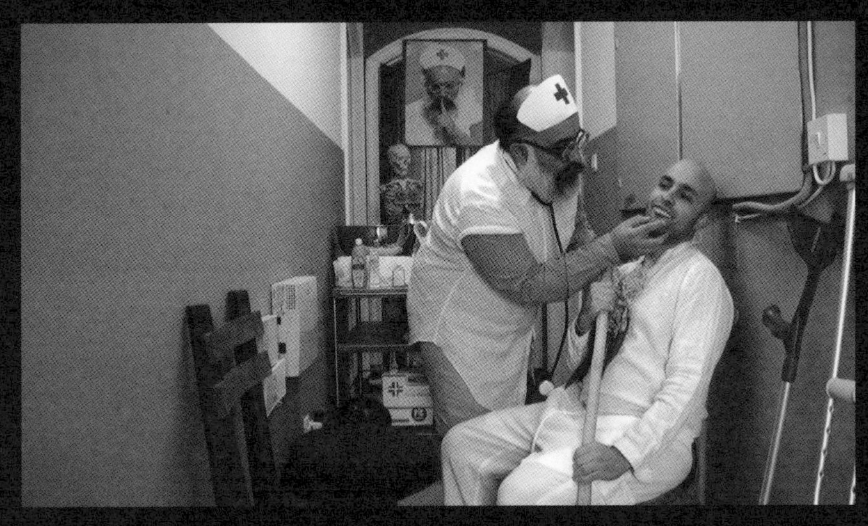

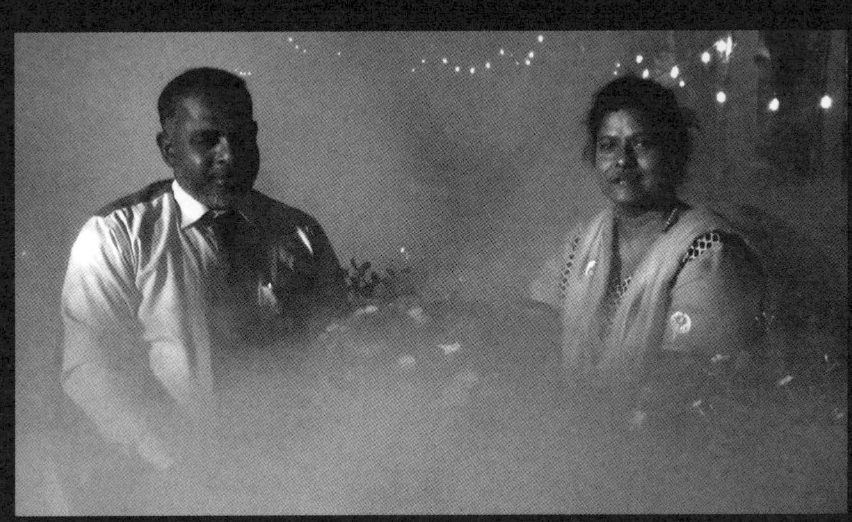

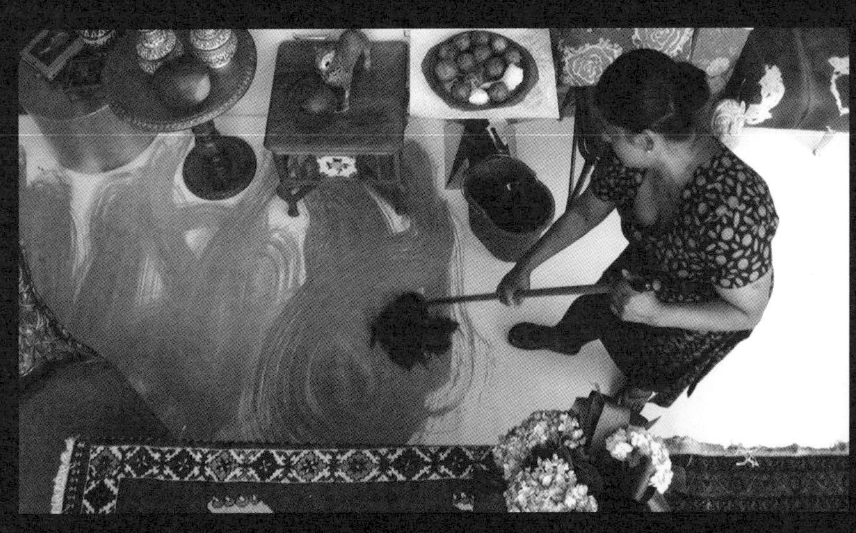

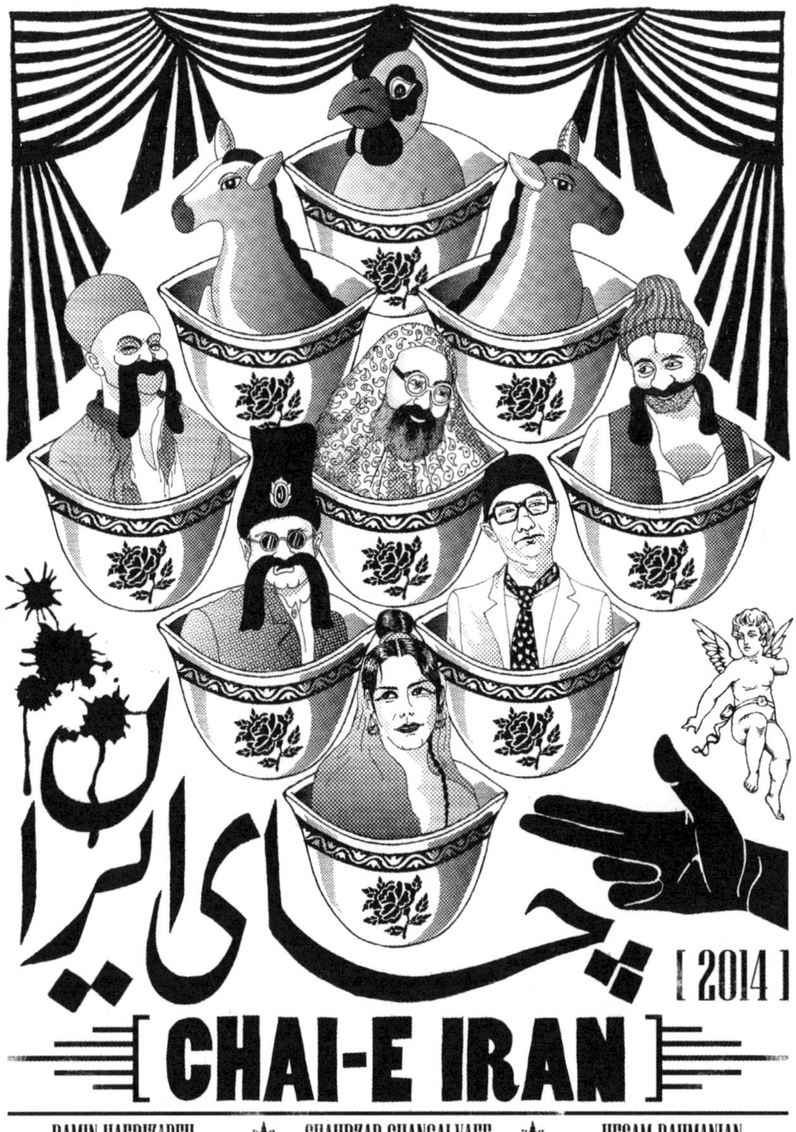

چای ای ایران
[2014]
[CHAI-E IRAN]
RAMIN HAERIZADEH
ROKNI HAERIZADEH
SHAHRZAD CHANGALVAEE
IMAN RAAD
HESAM RAHMANIAN
MAZIAR SADR

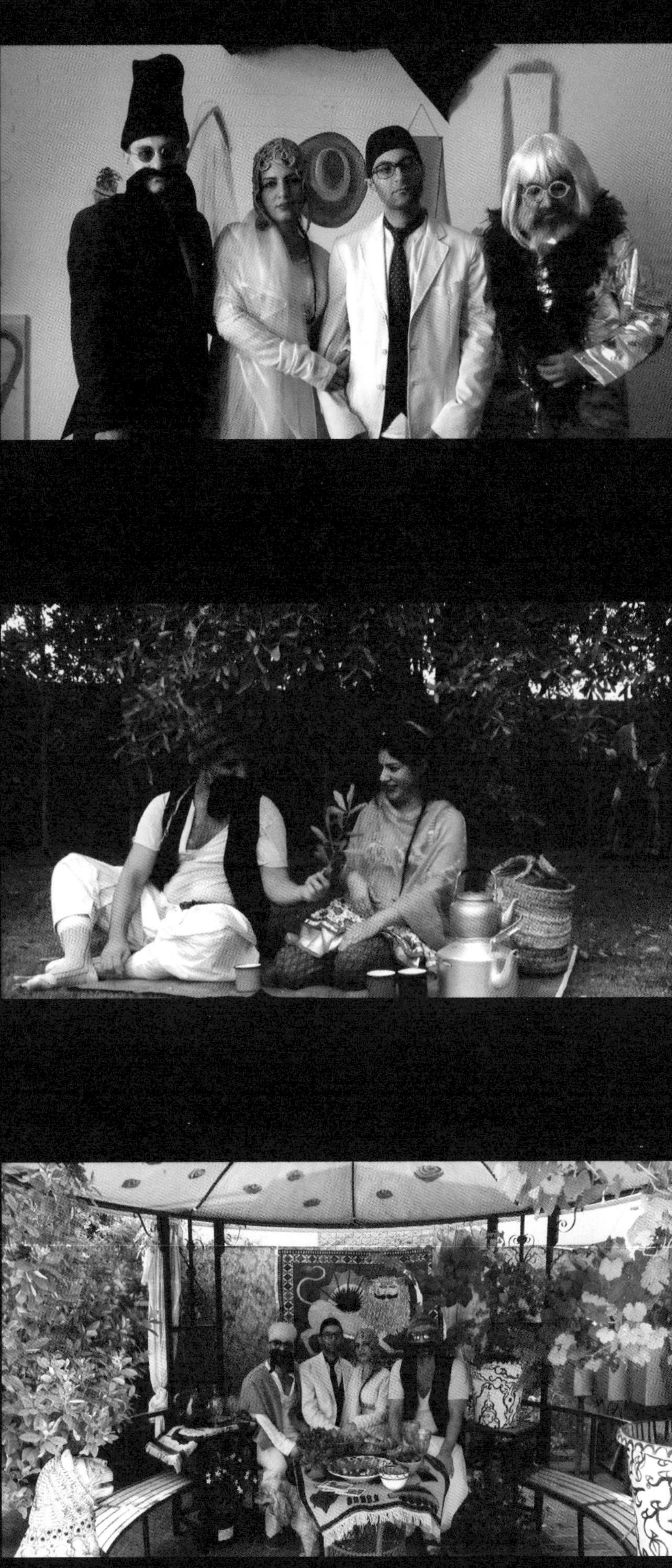

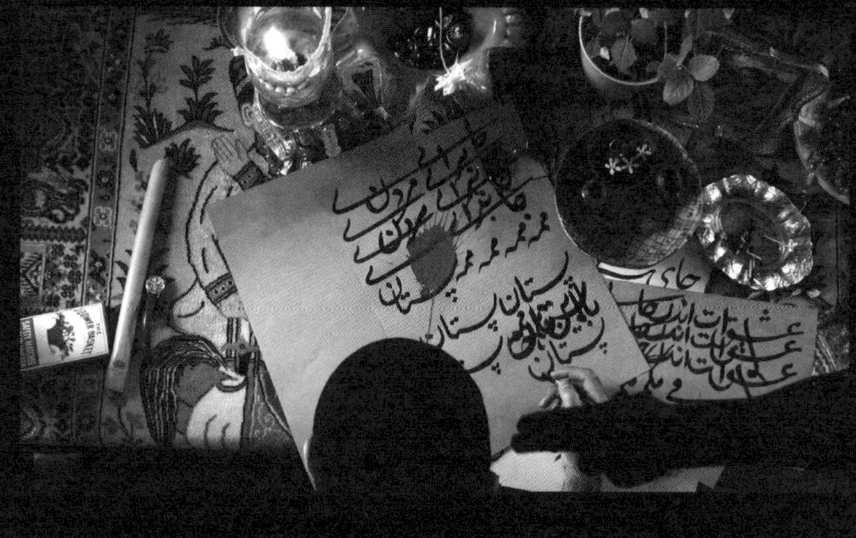

Chai-e Iran, 2013 – 2014
Featuring Iman Raad. Shahrzad Changalvaee. Maaziar Sadr
26′ 39″

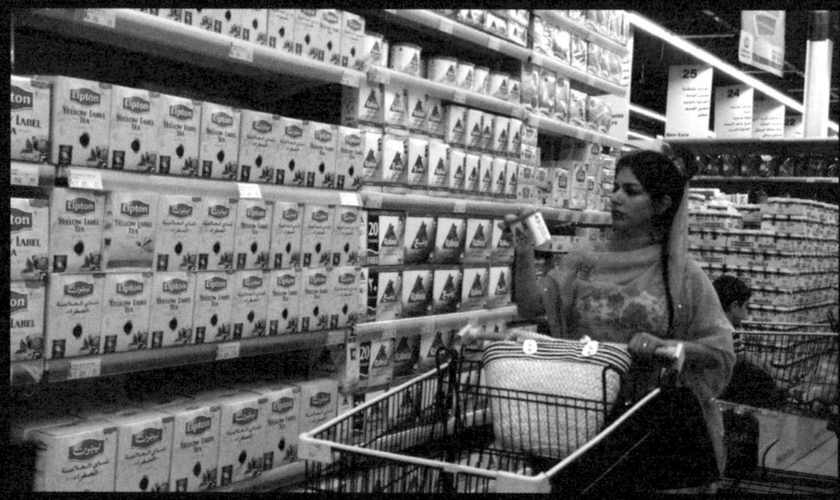

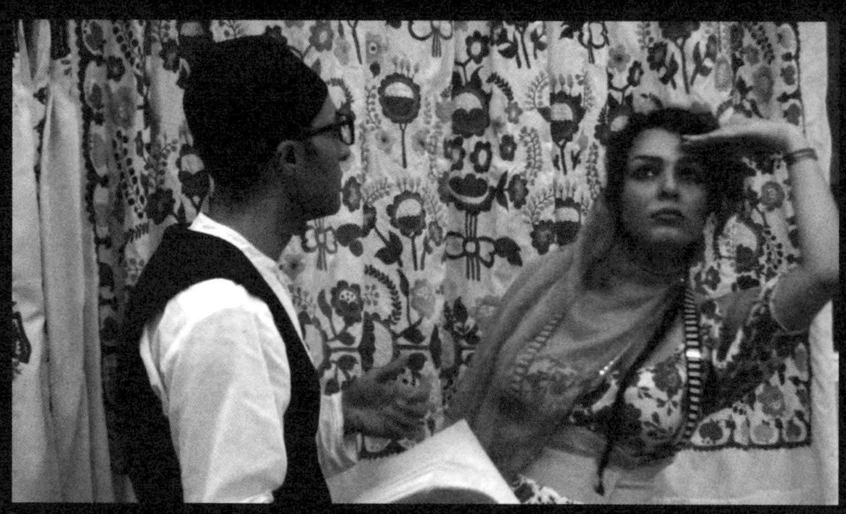

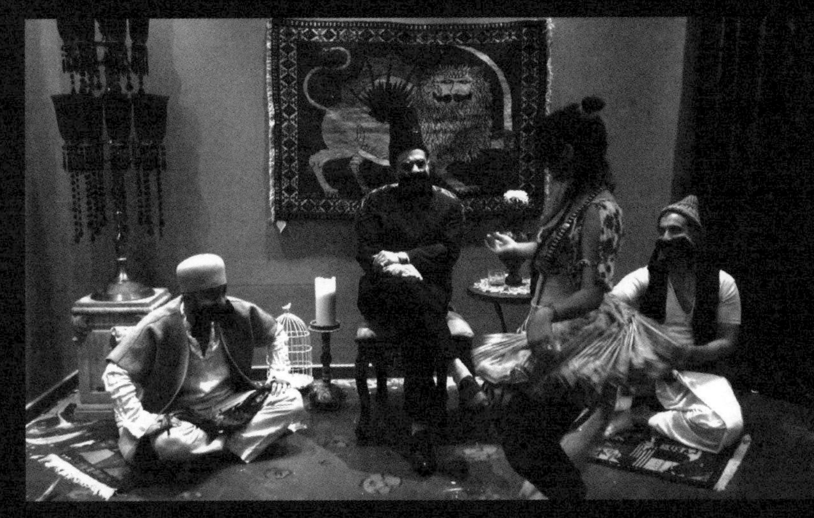

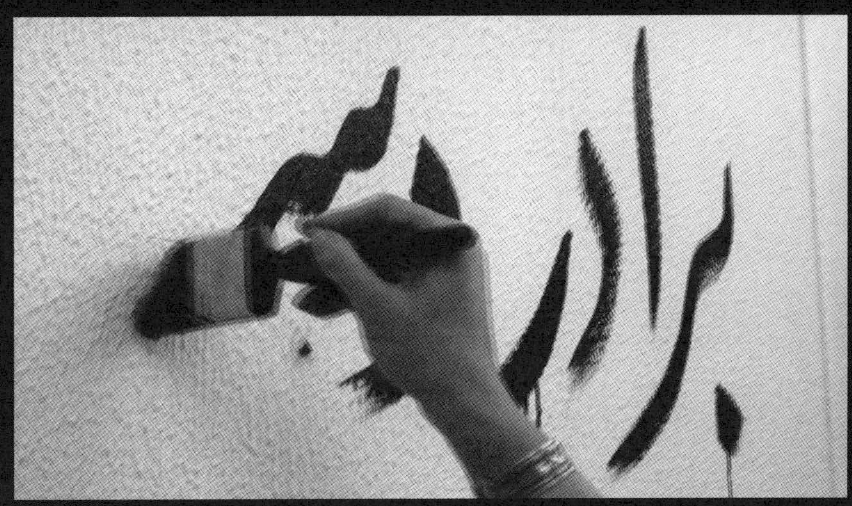
برای

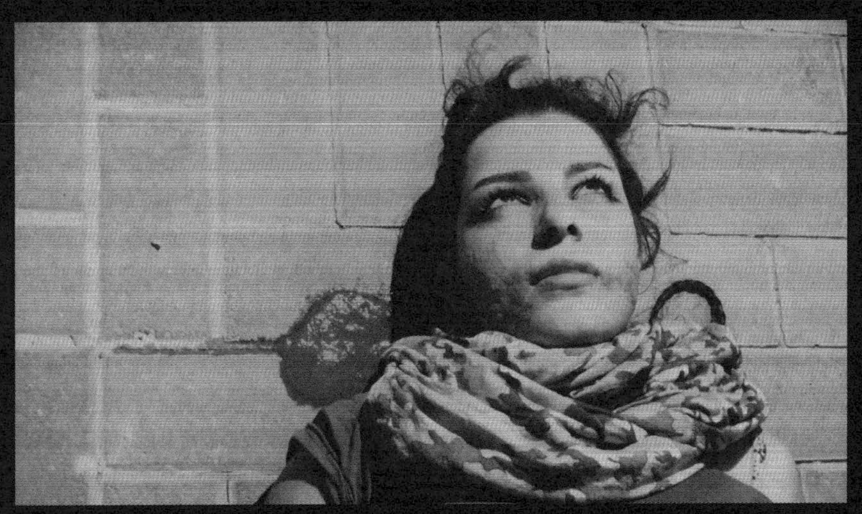

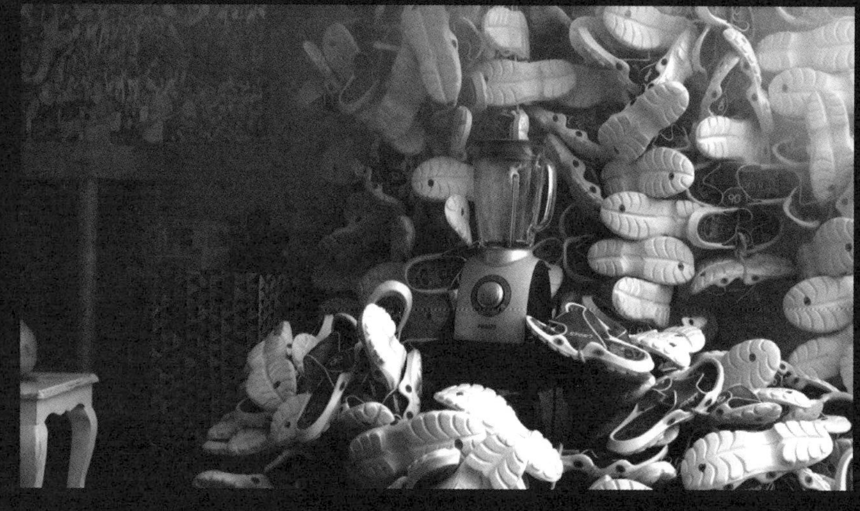

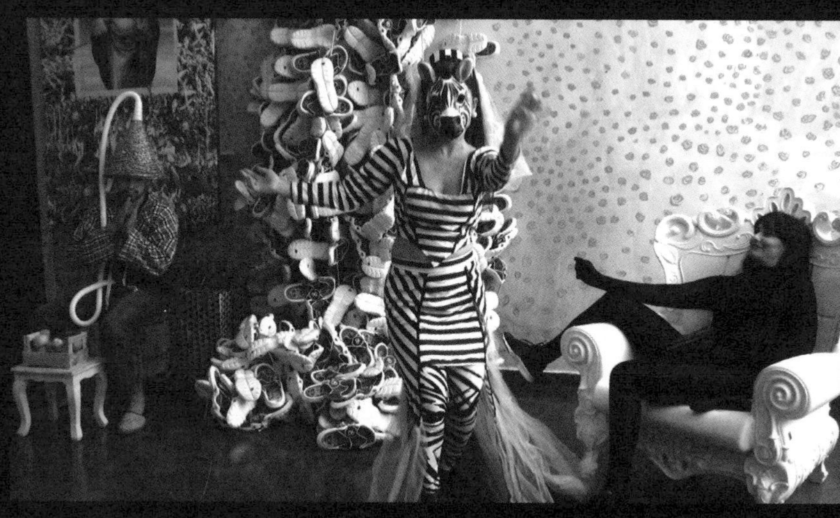

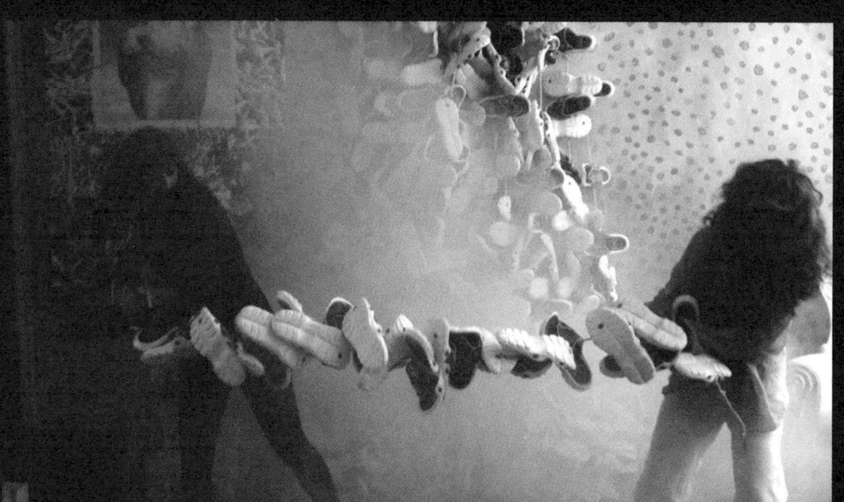

Foolad. 2014 – 2015
Featuring Nazli Ghassemi. Nesa Azadikhah. Niyaz Azadikhah. Maaziar Sadr
19' 30''

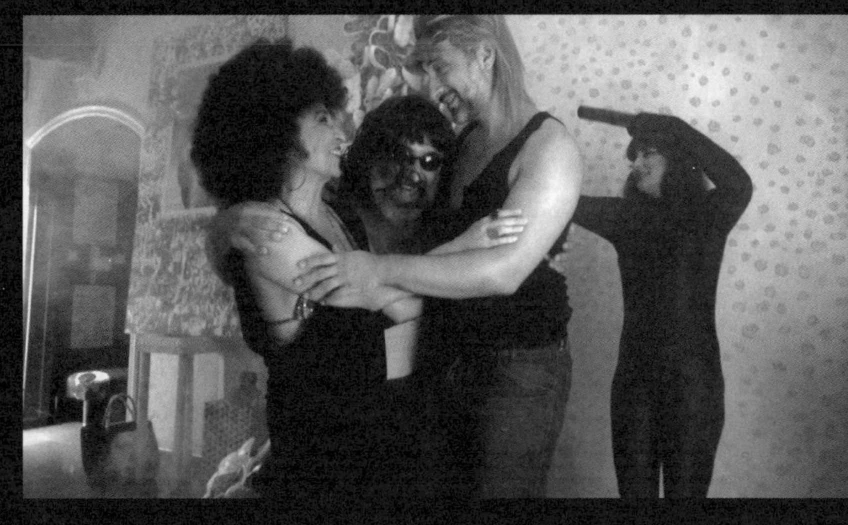

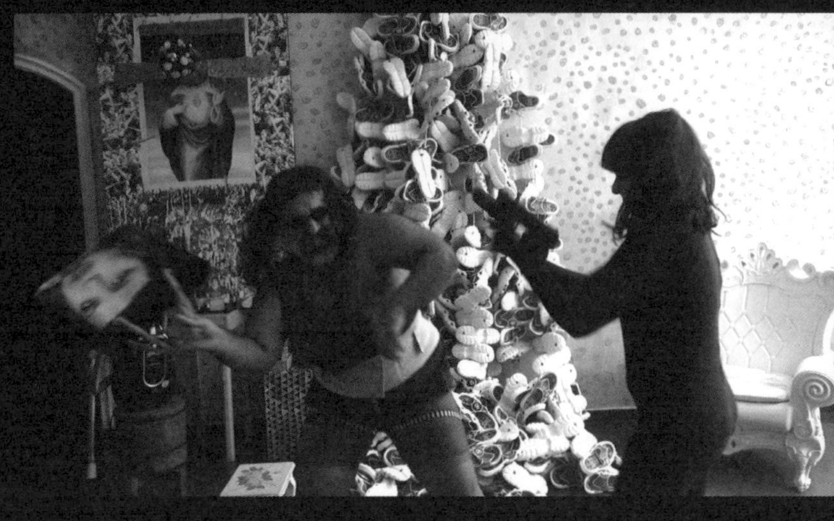

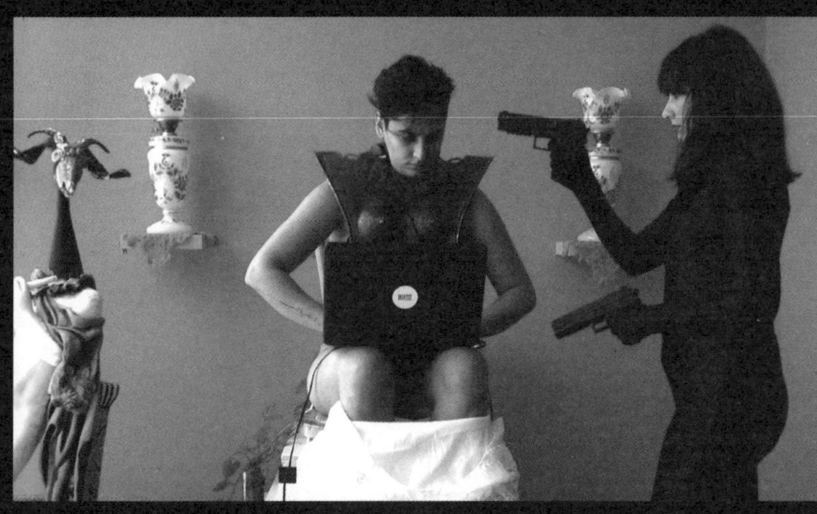

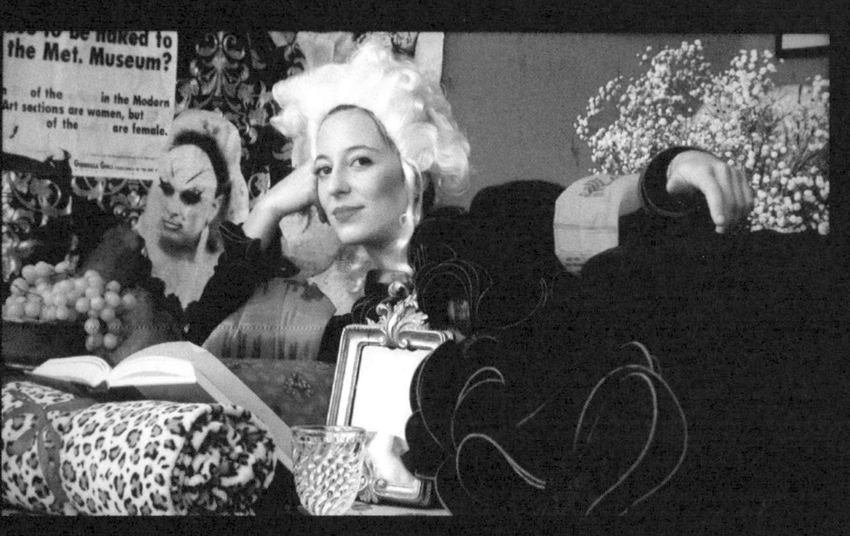
to be naked to
the Met. Museum?
of the   in the Modern
Art sections are women, but
of the   are female.
Guerrilla Girls

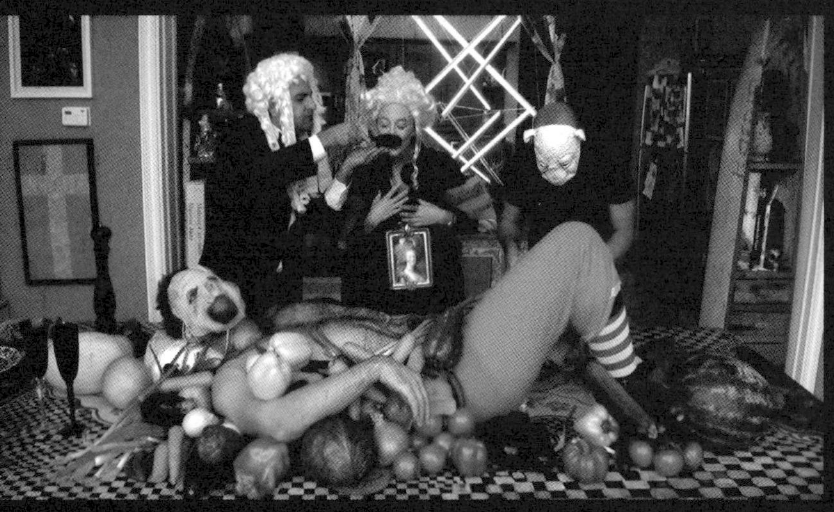

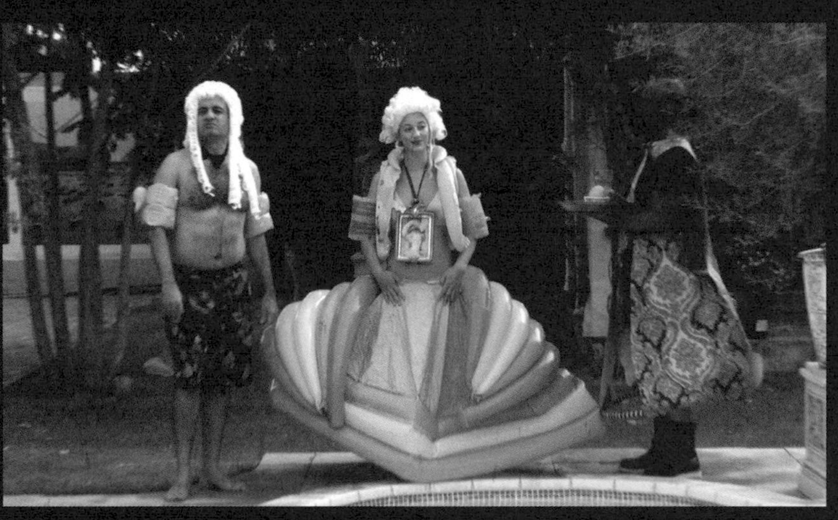

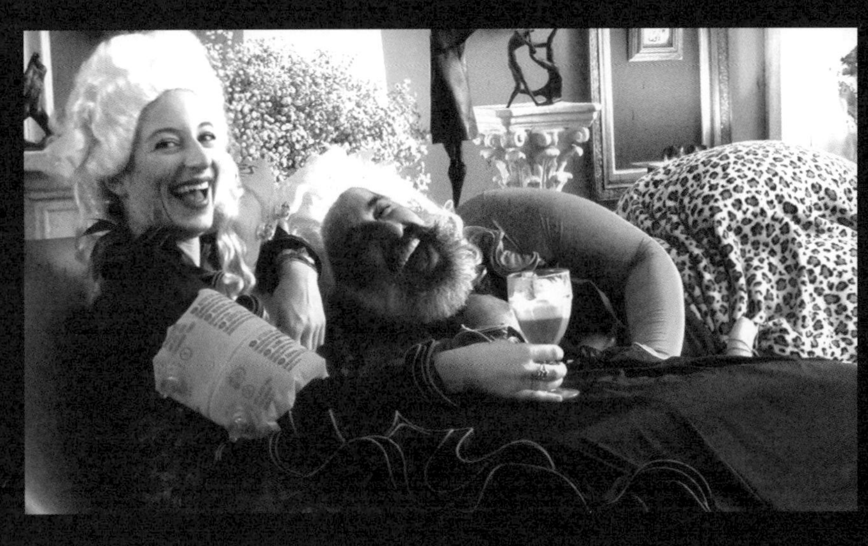

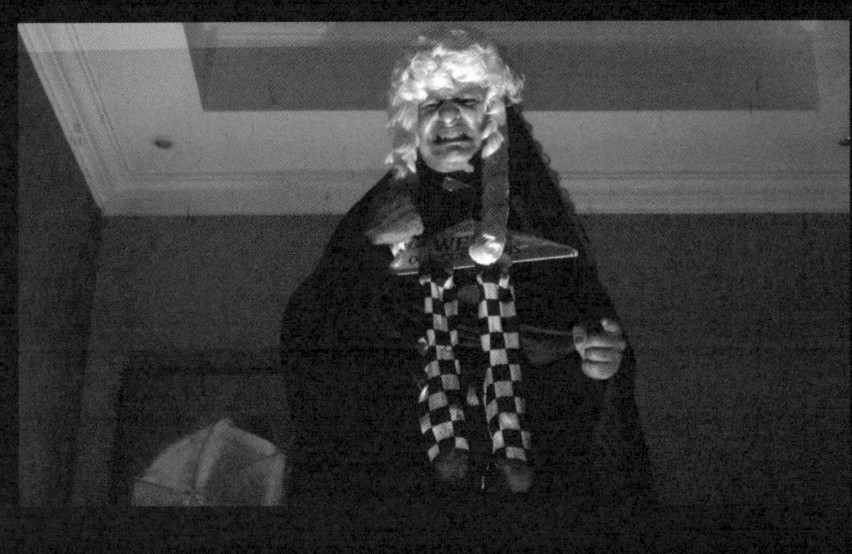

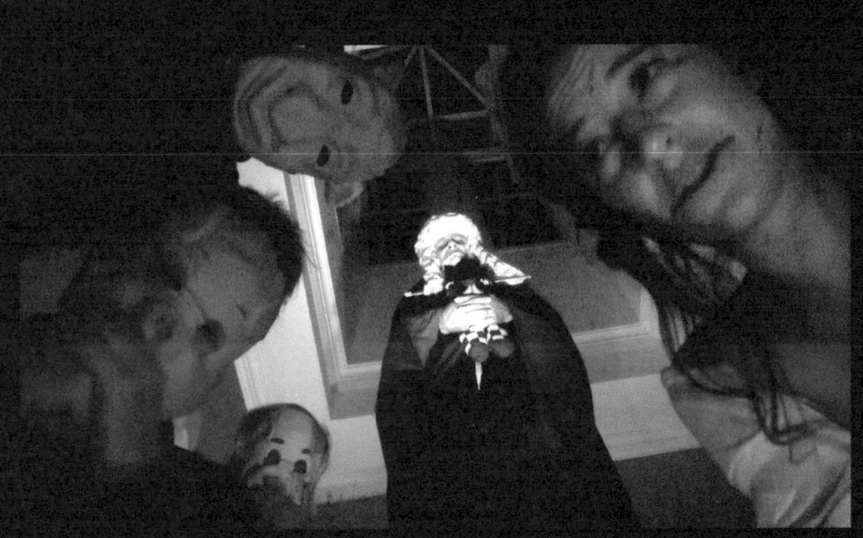

I.

O you people, who are seated, cheerful and
laughing,
    on the shore
Someone is losing his life in the water;
Someone is flailing in the rough, dark
    and formidable sea.

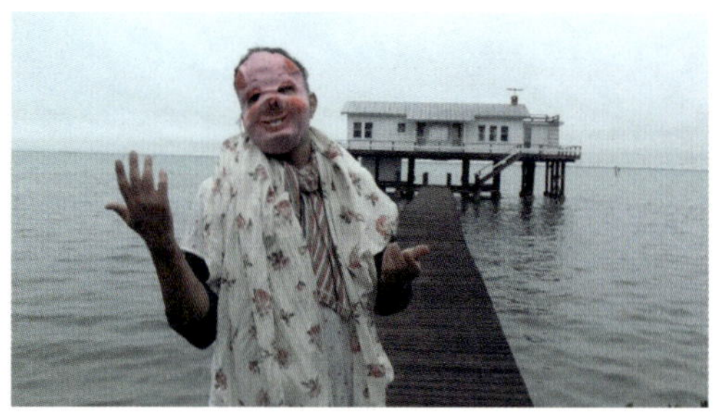

II.

Just when you're drunk on thoughts
    of disarming your enemies,
When you tell yourselves
That to hold one feeble hand
Is to relieve the suffering of all.
The times when you gird up your loins
    for some pursuit.

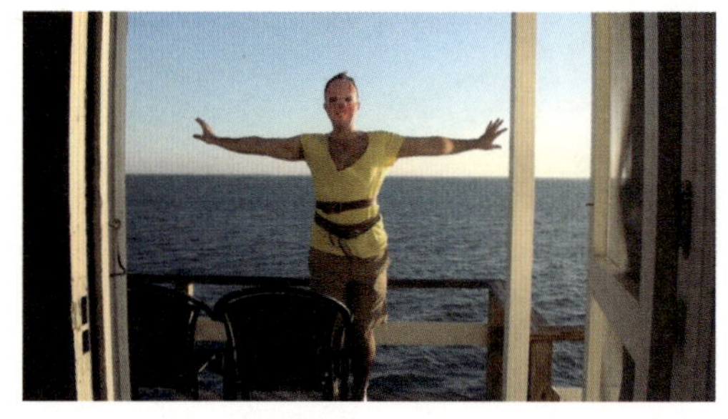

III.

When is it a good time to say
That a life is fading to a futile end in the sea.
    O you people, exhilarated on the shore:
Your tables bountiful, your bodies well-
    clothed;
Someone in the water is calling you.

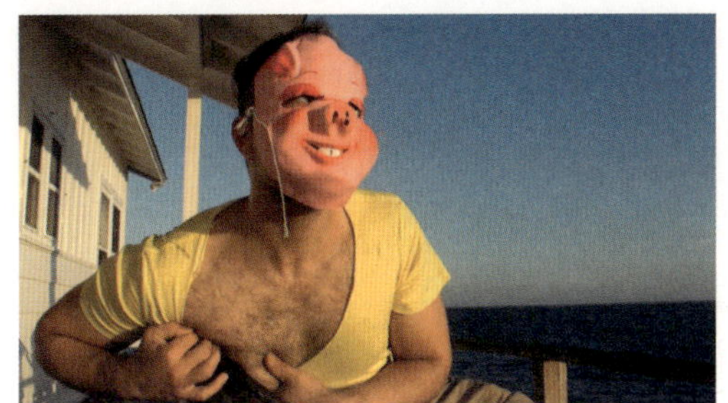 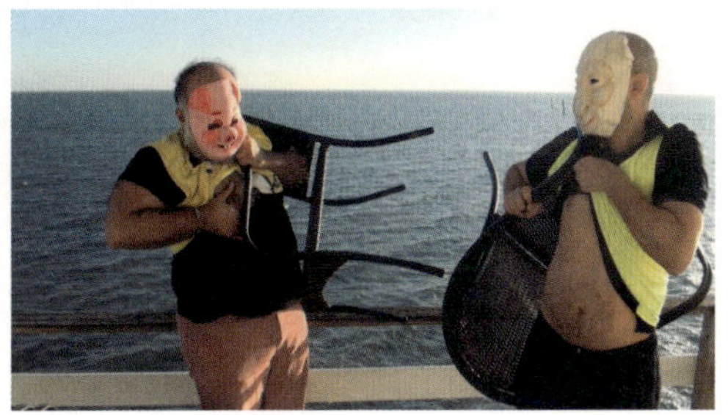

IV.

He is beating the heavy waves with
exhausted hands.
He is gasping for breath, his eyes torn
    with terror;
He has seen your shadow in the distance.
But water has filled his insides amid
    the deep
And as each moment brings no relief
Out of the water he thrusts
Now his head, Now his feet.
"O you people!"

V.

He tries to keep sight
    of this worn world from afar,
And hoping for help, he cries out;
O you people, who enjoy the view
    from the tranquil shore!

VI.

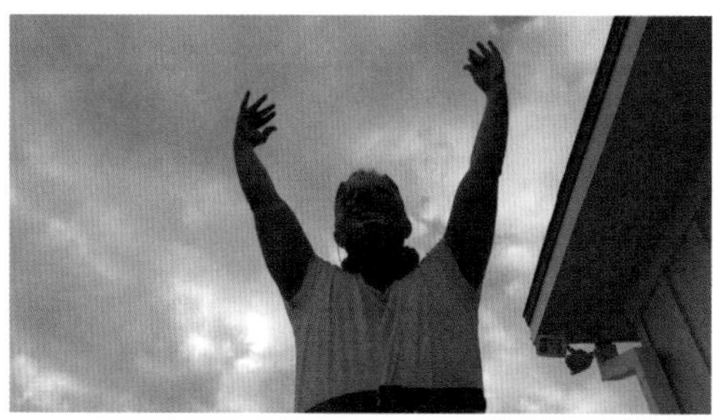

The waves rush in and thump on the
    silent shore,
Fall like a drunk,
Sprawled on the bed, unconscious,
And then roar as they retreat into the sea.
Again the same cry comes from far away:
"O you people…"

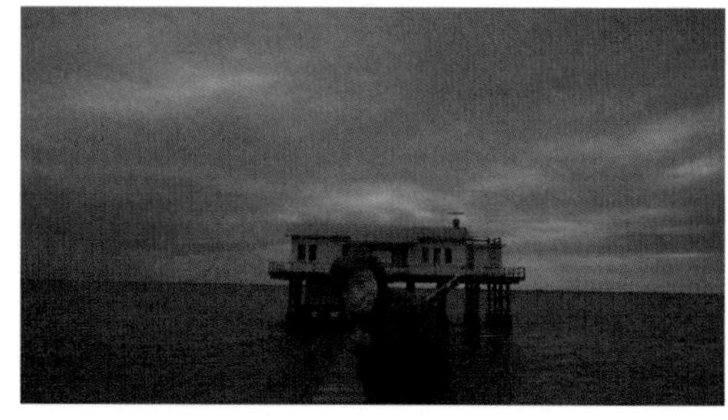

VII.

And the wind bellows a tormenting sound,
And the man's cry spreads out over the sea,
  riding the wind's howl,
And from the midst of the water,
  near and far
Again his sigh echoes:
"O you people. . ."

Originally 'Ay Adamha', 1941, by Nima Yushij.
Unfaithfully translated as O You People in 2014
by Nazli Ghassemi and Christopher Lord

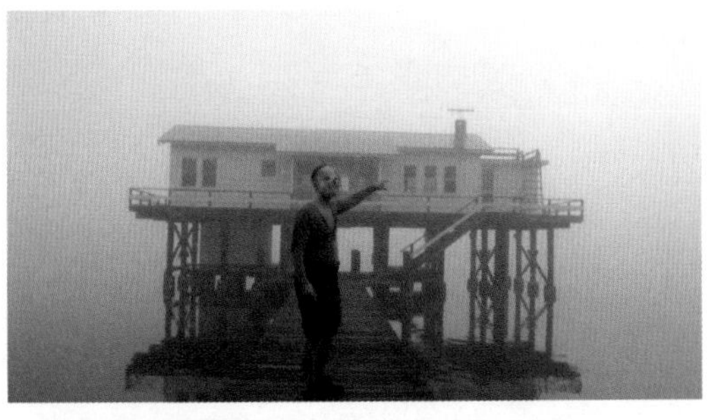

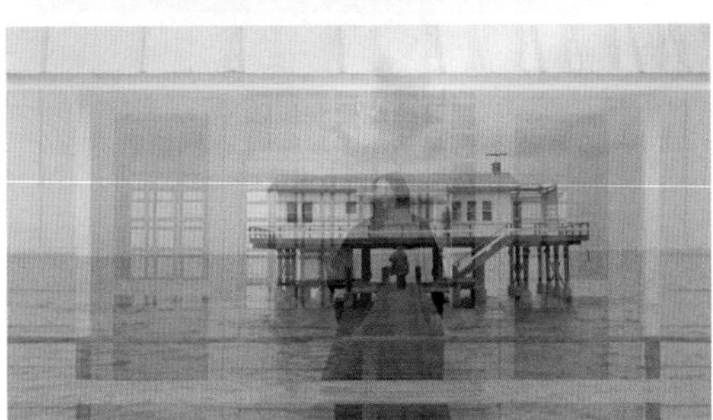

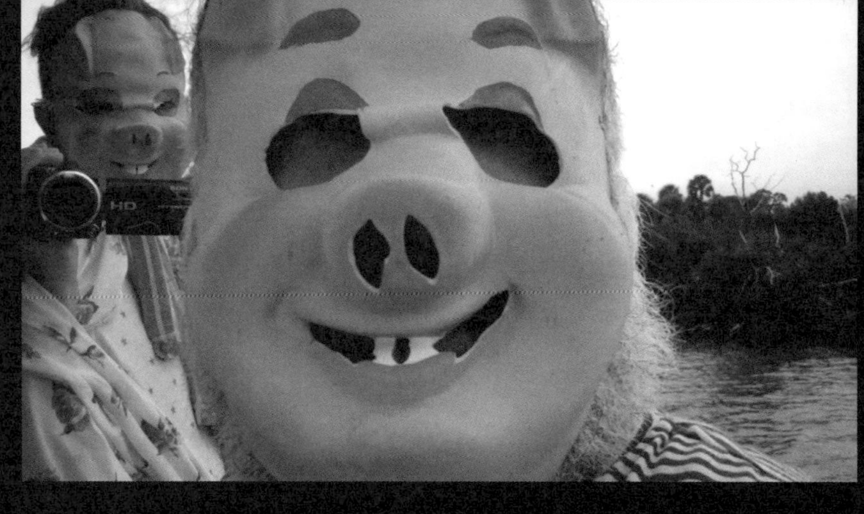

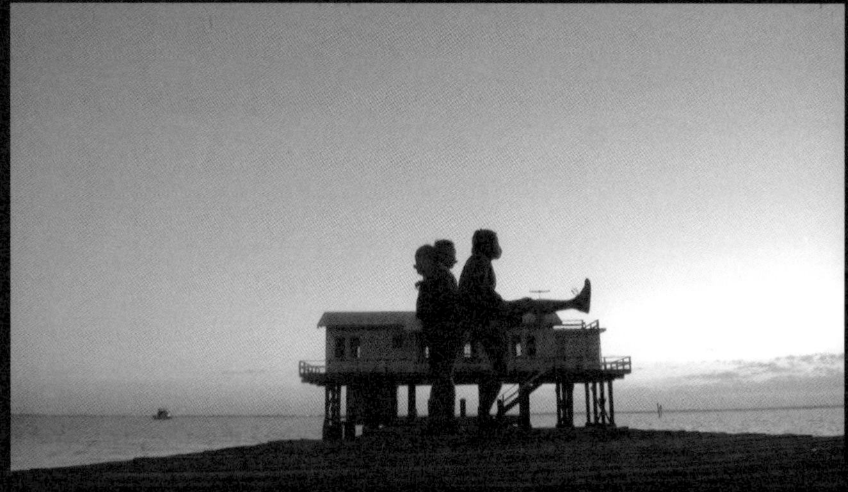

O, You People!, 2014
Featuring Minnie McIntyre and Christopher Lord
1 hour 39"

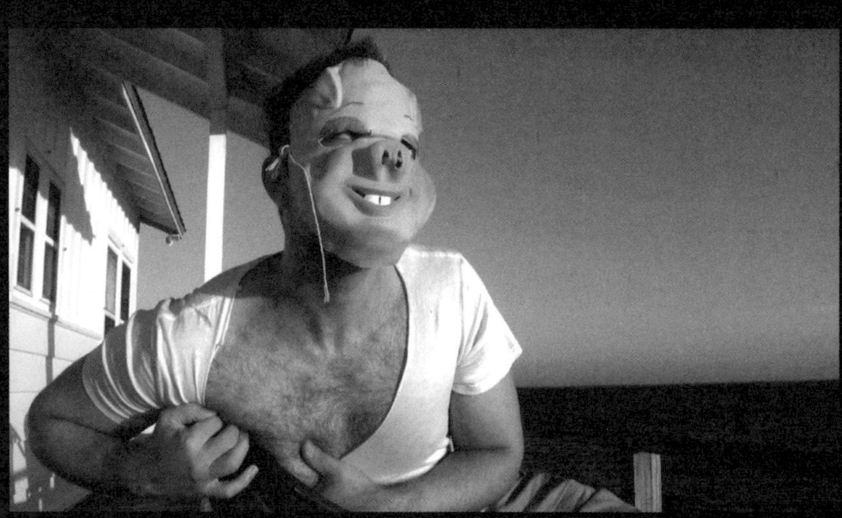

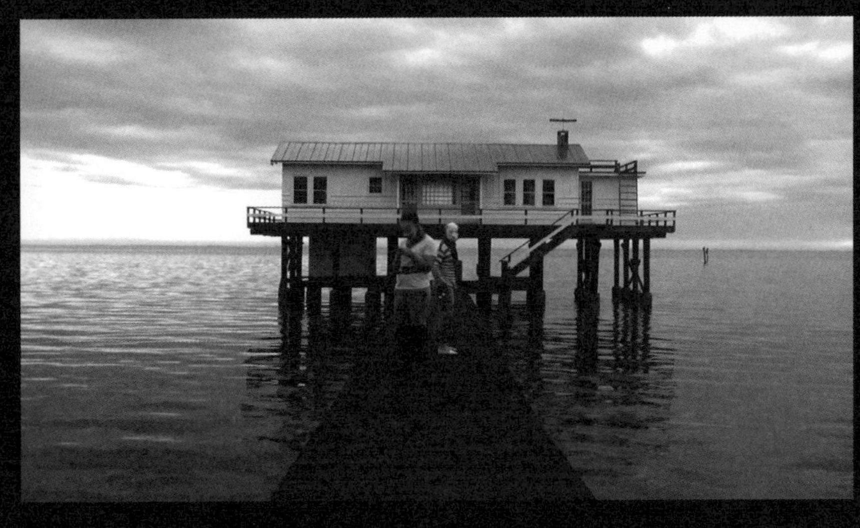

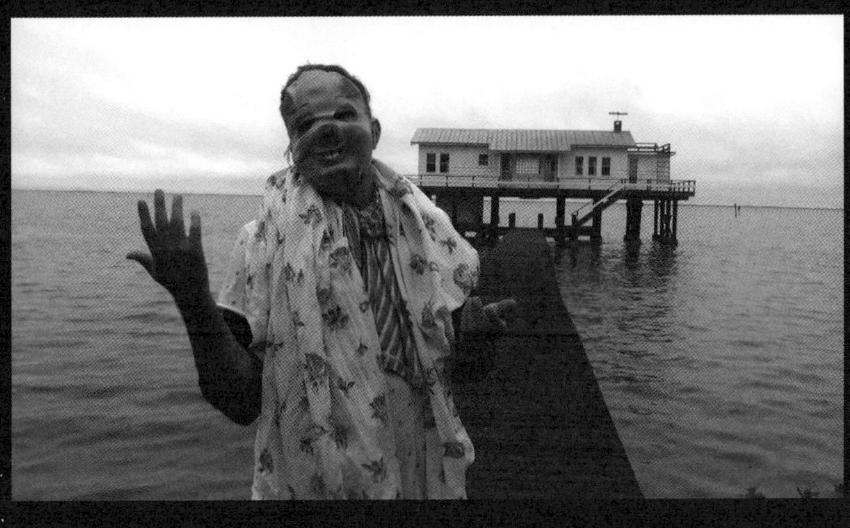

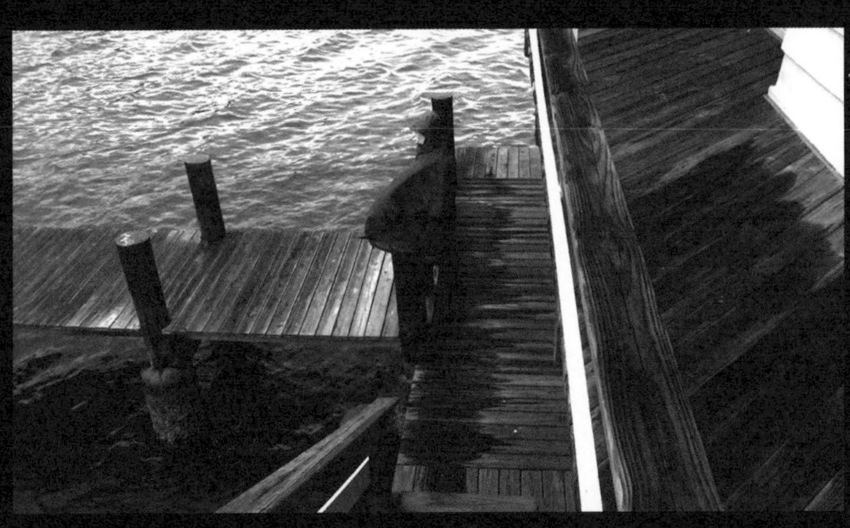

INSTALLATION VIEWS
I Put It There You Name It, 2012
The Exquisite Corpse Shall Drink the New Wine, 2014
Gallery Isabelle van den Eynde, Dubai

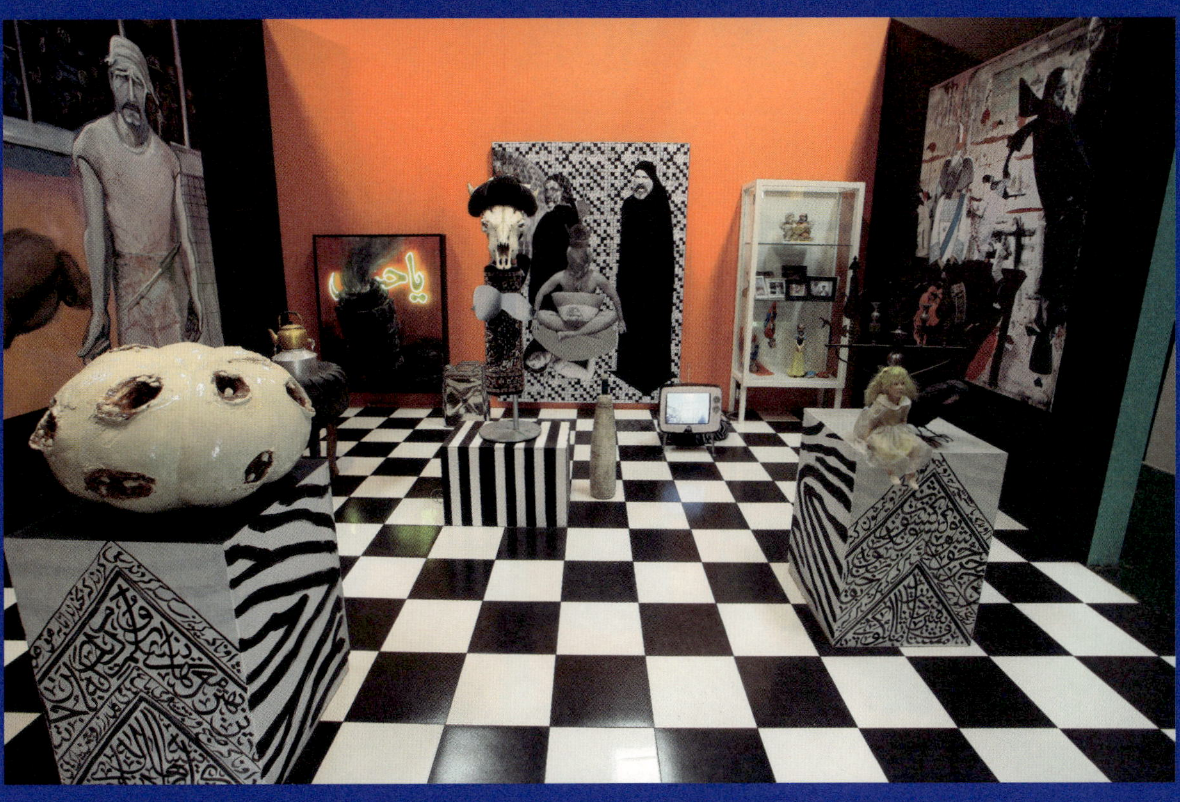

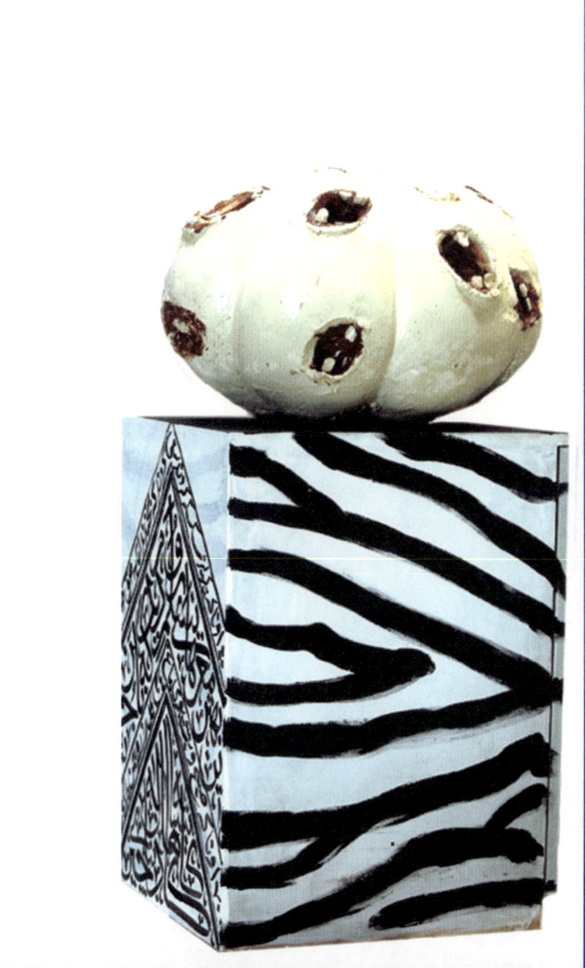

Installation view, *The Exquisite Corpse Shall Drink the New Wine*, 2014.
Rokni Haerizadeh, *Screaming Pumpkin*, 2010. Plinth by Iman Raad
Glazed ceramic
38 x Ø60 cm

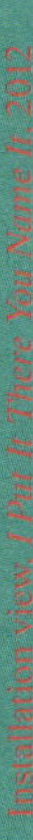

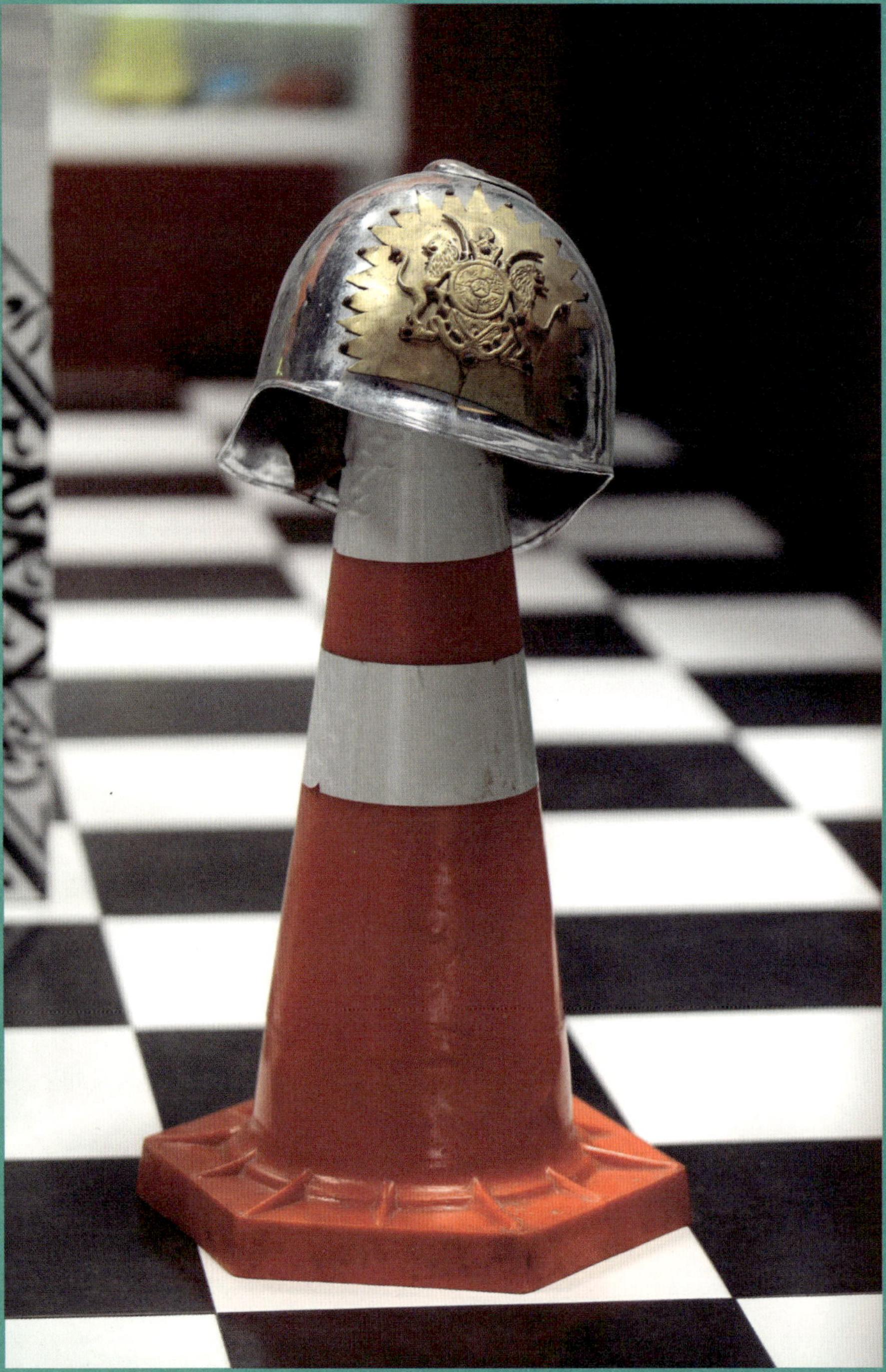

Installation view, *I Put It There You Name It*, 2012

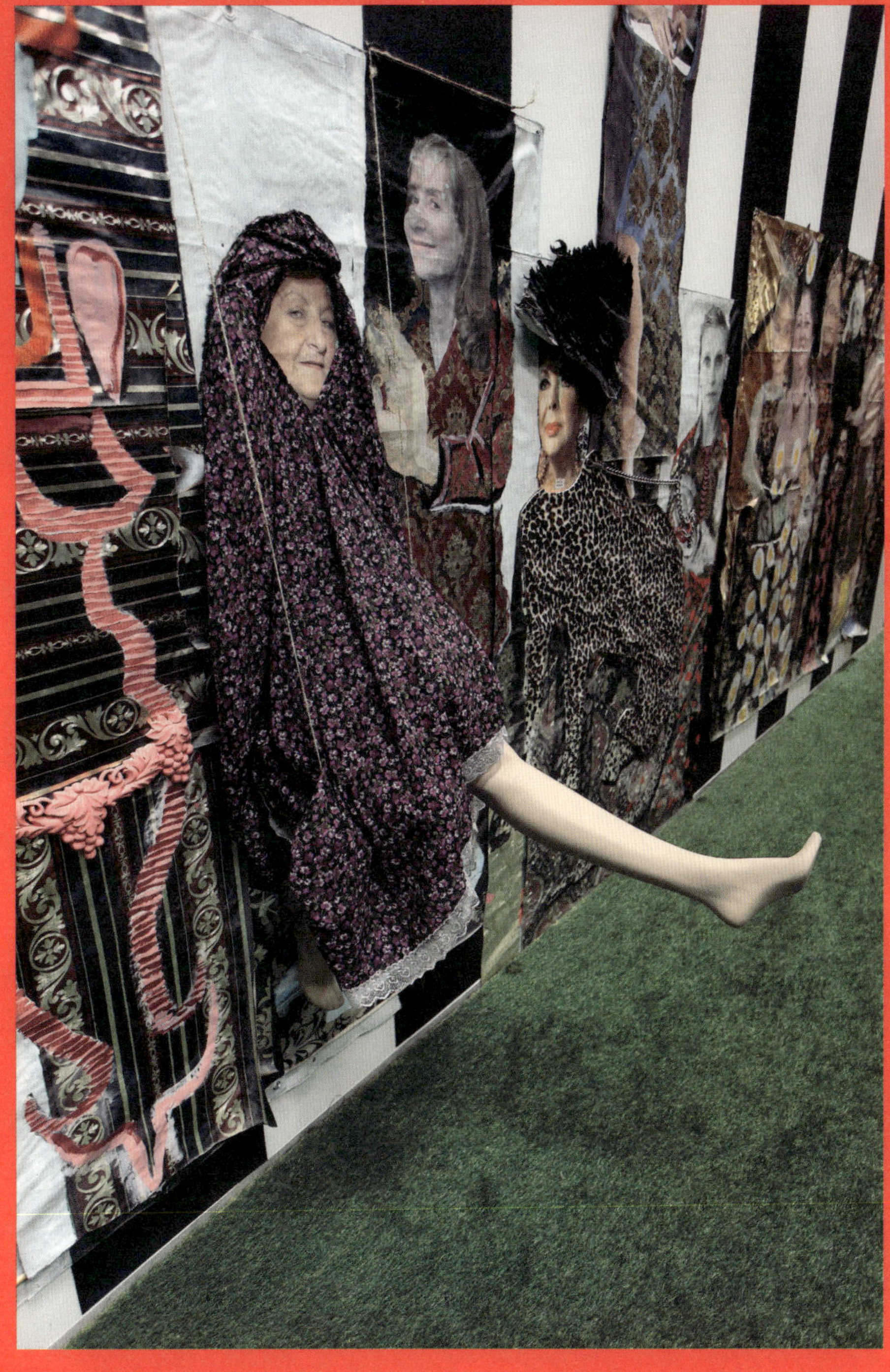

Installation view, *I Put It There You Name It*, 2012
Garden of Grandmothers 04 (detail), 2014
Wallpaper, paper collage, acrylic, stings, fibreglass mannequin body parts,
wood, feathers, chain and fabrics on plastic tarp
300 x 540 x 83 cm

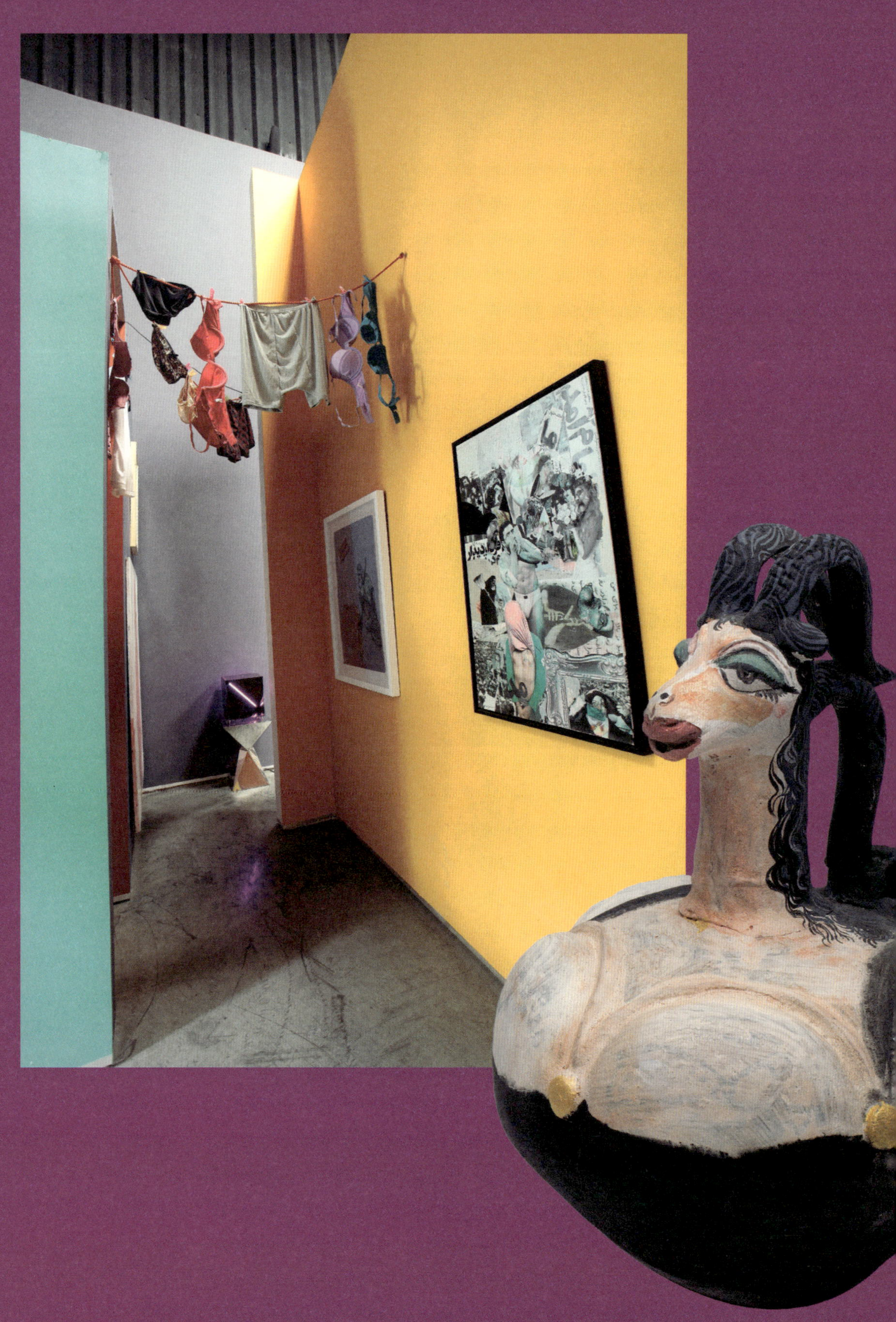

92

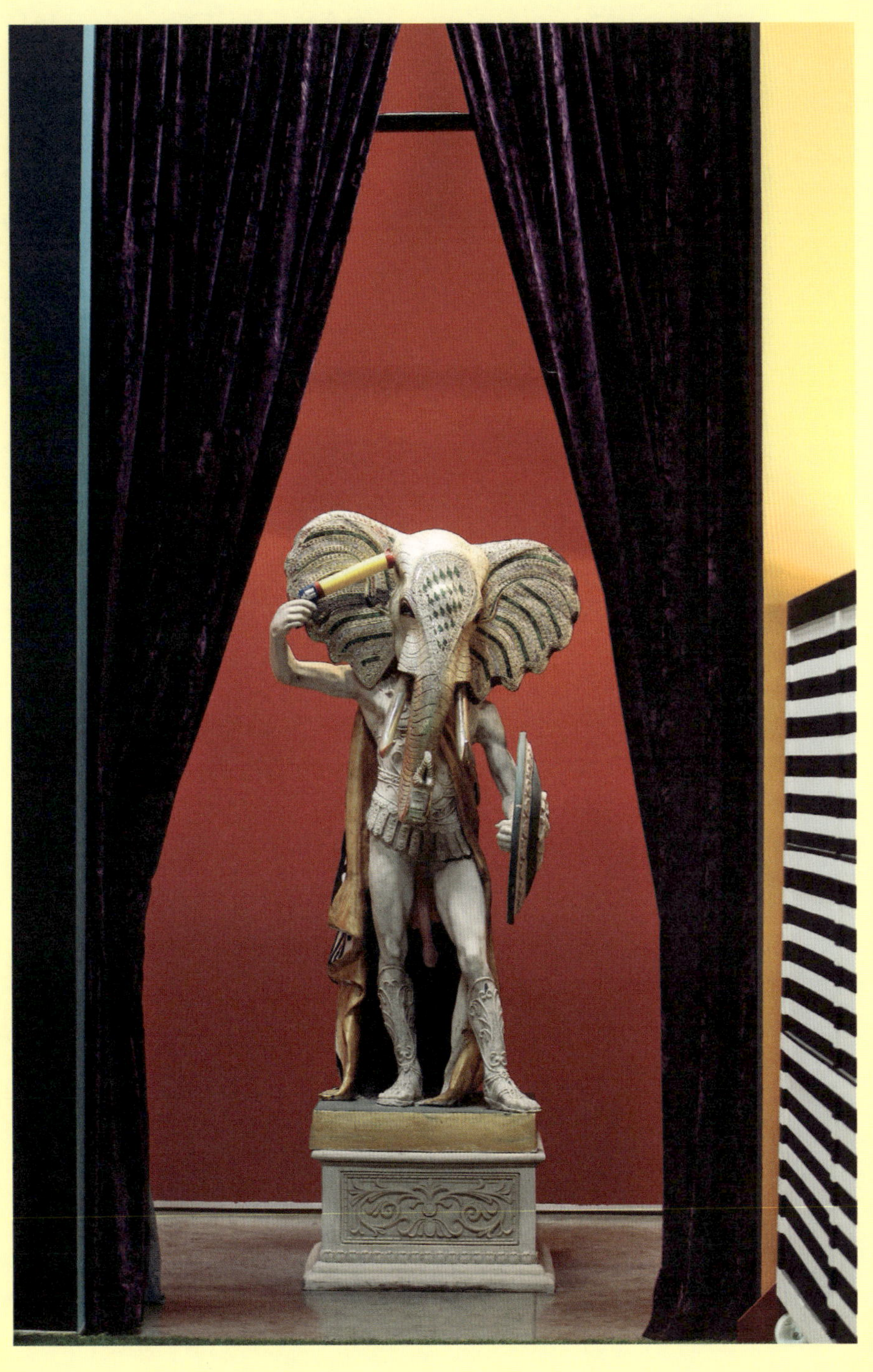

Installation view, *I Put It There You Name It*, 2012
Ganesh, 2012

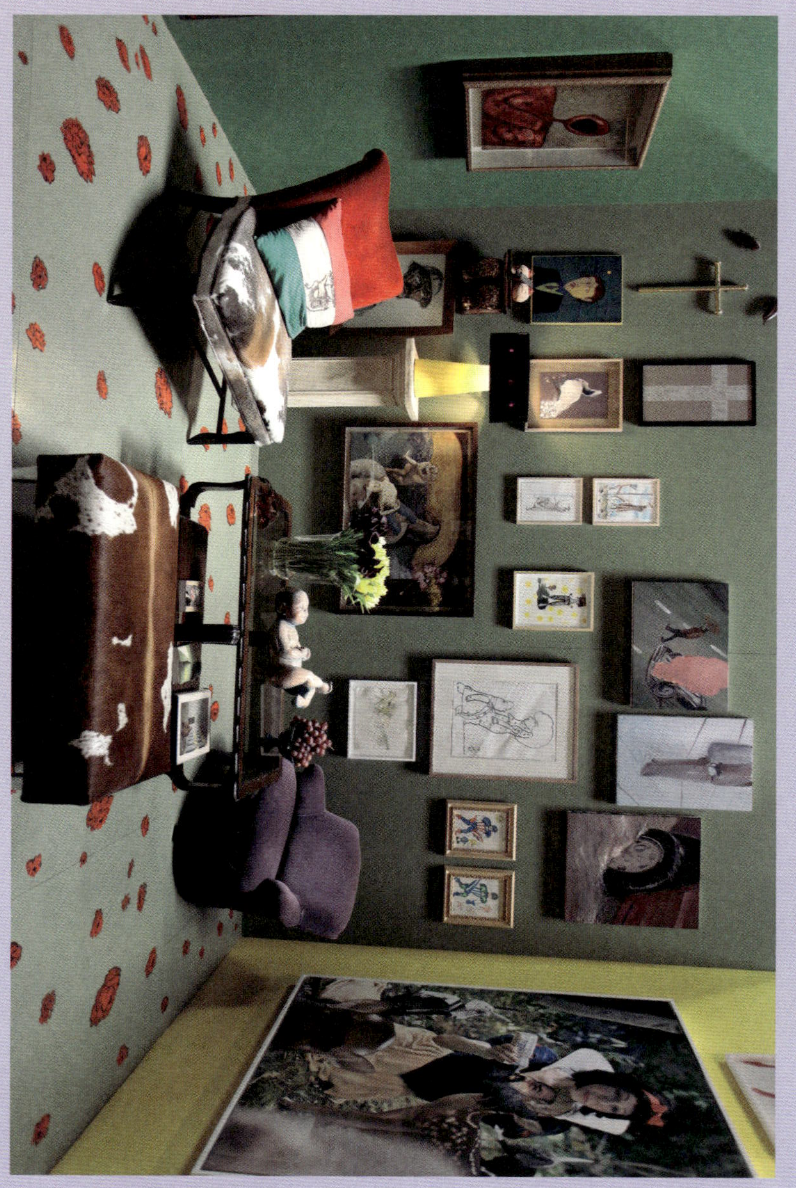

Installation view, *I Put It There You Name It*, 2012
Including works from right to left, top to bottom: Bahmar: Mohasses, Bita Fayyazi, Shahpour Pouyan, Adel Auer, Shirin Fakhim, Houshang Pezeshknia, Y Z Kami, Rokni Haerizadeh, Nader Ahriman, Rokni Haerizadeh, triptych by Hesam Rahmanian, Ramin Haerizadeh, Ardeshir Mohasses, Avish Khebrehzadeh, Daniel Johnston. On the table, *Baby*, 2009, by Bita Fayyazi

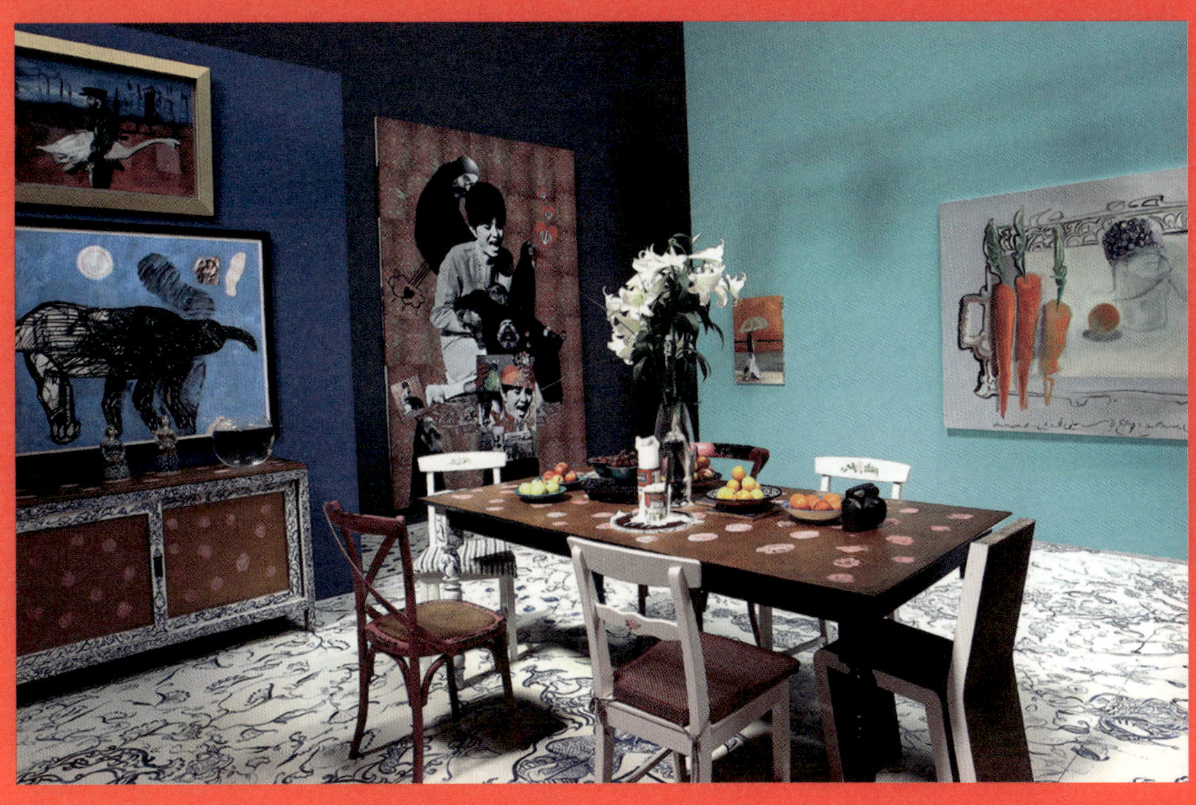

Installation view. *I Put It There You Name It*, 2012
Including from left to right: Hesam Rahmanian, *Captured Swan*, 2011; Farshid Maleki, *Untitled*, 2009; Ramin Haerizadeh, *Hail to the King*, 2011; Hesam Rahmanian, *The Savior*, 2012; Rokni Haerizadeh, *Still Life. Three Carrots, Bergamot and an Old Tray*, 2009

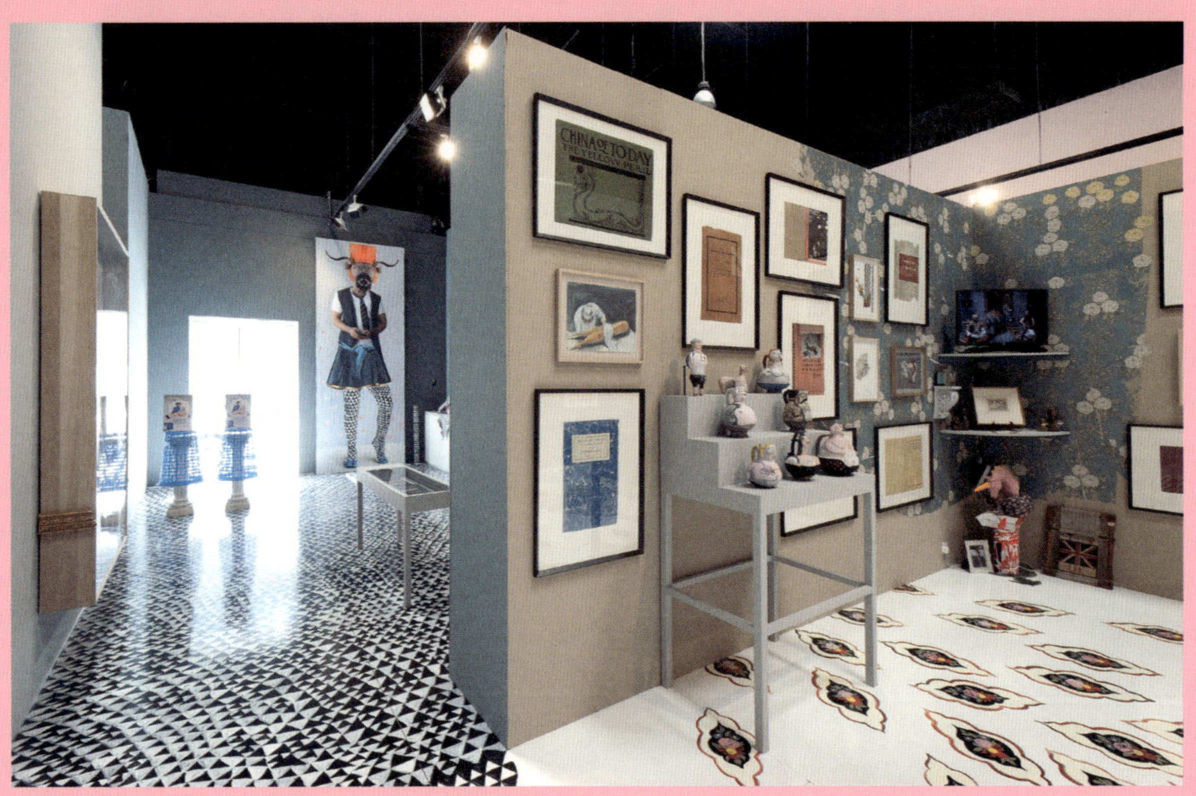

Installation view, *The Exquisite Corpse Shall Drink the New Wine*, 2014

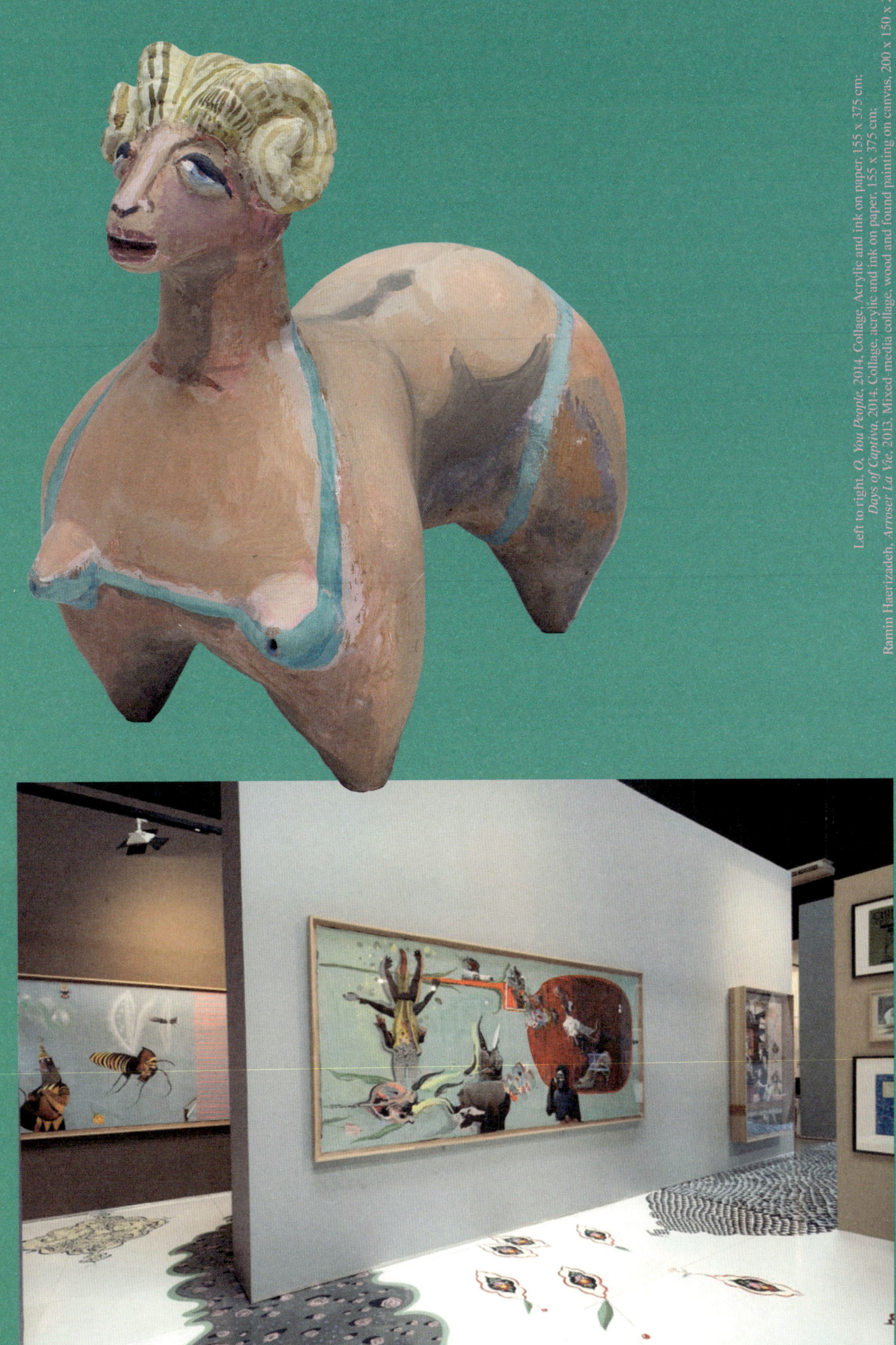

Left to right. *O, You People*, 2014, Collage. Acrylic and ink on paper, 155 x 375 cm; *Days of Cupiva*, 2014, Collage, acrylic and ink on paper, 155 x 375 cm; Ramin Haerizadeh, *Arroser La Vie*, 2013, Mixed-media collage, wood and found painting on canvas, 200 x 150 x 25 cm

Installation view. *The Exquisite Corpse Shall Drink the New Wine*, 2014

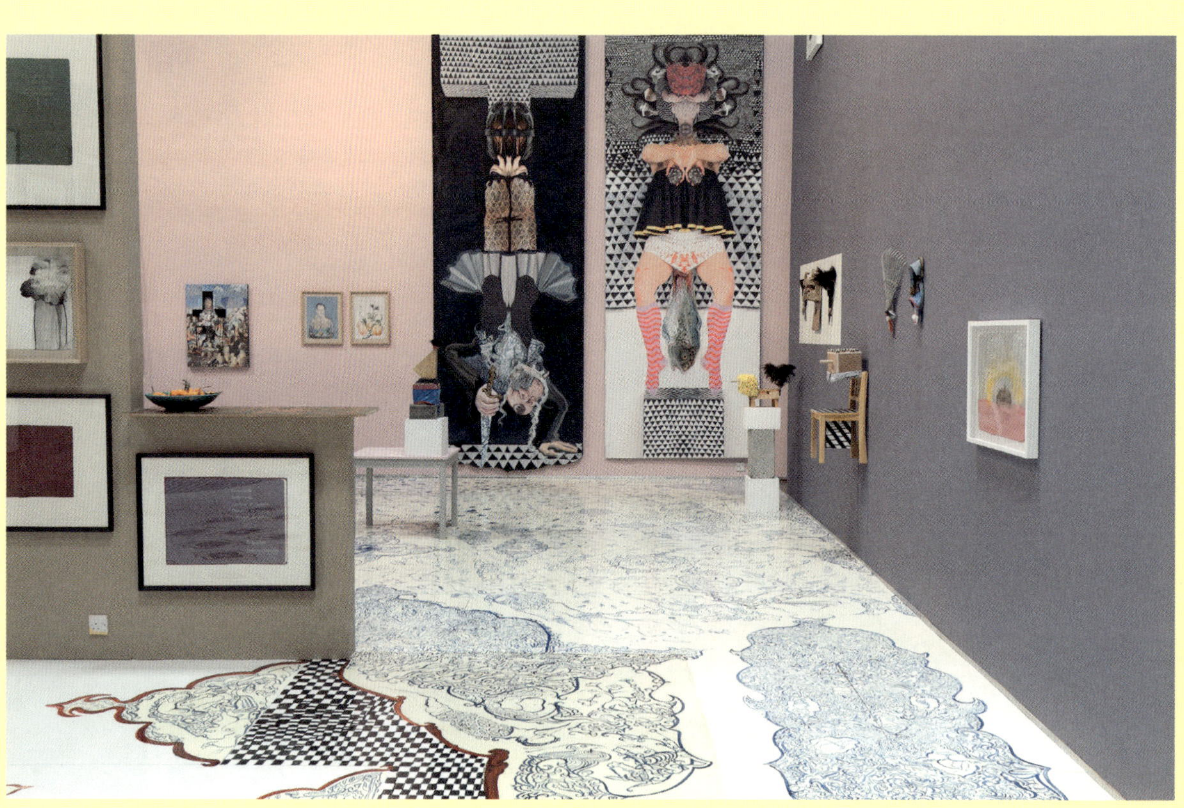

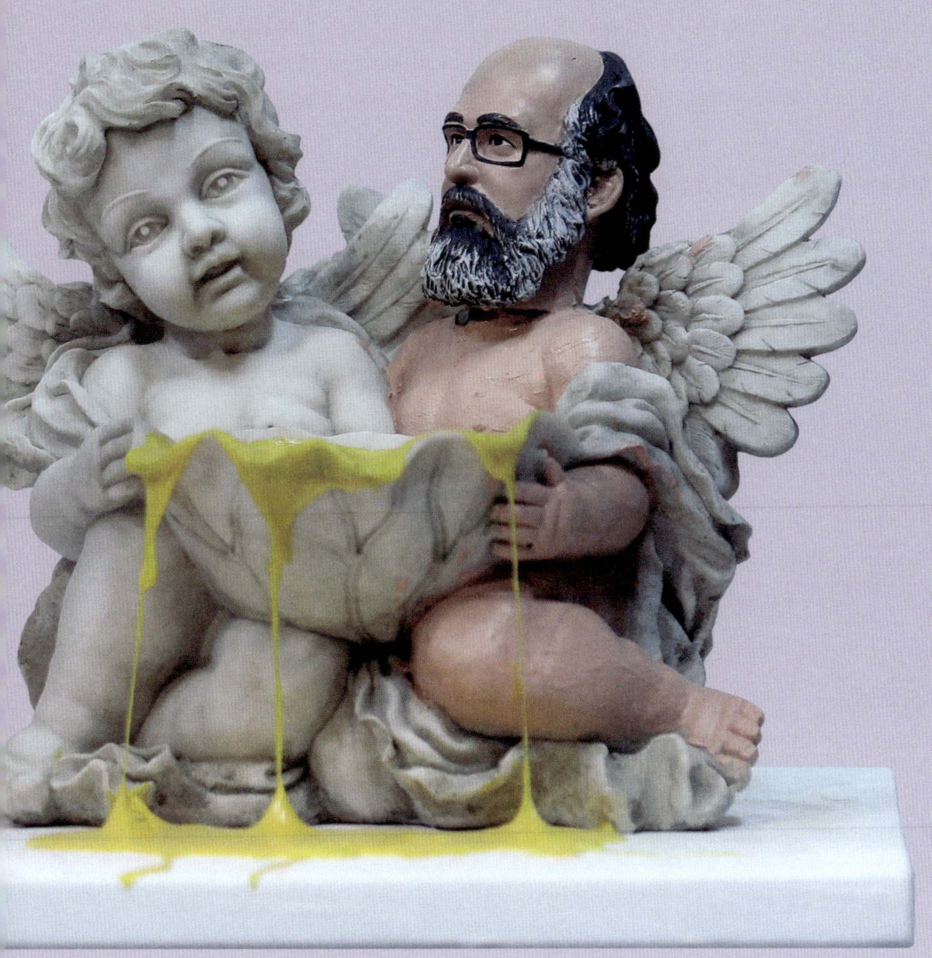

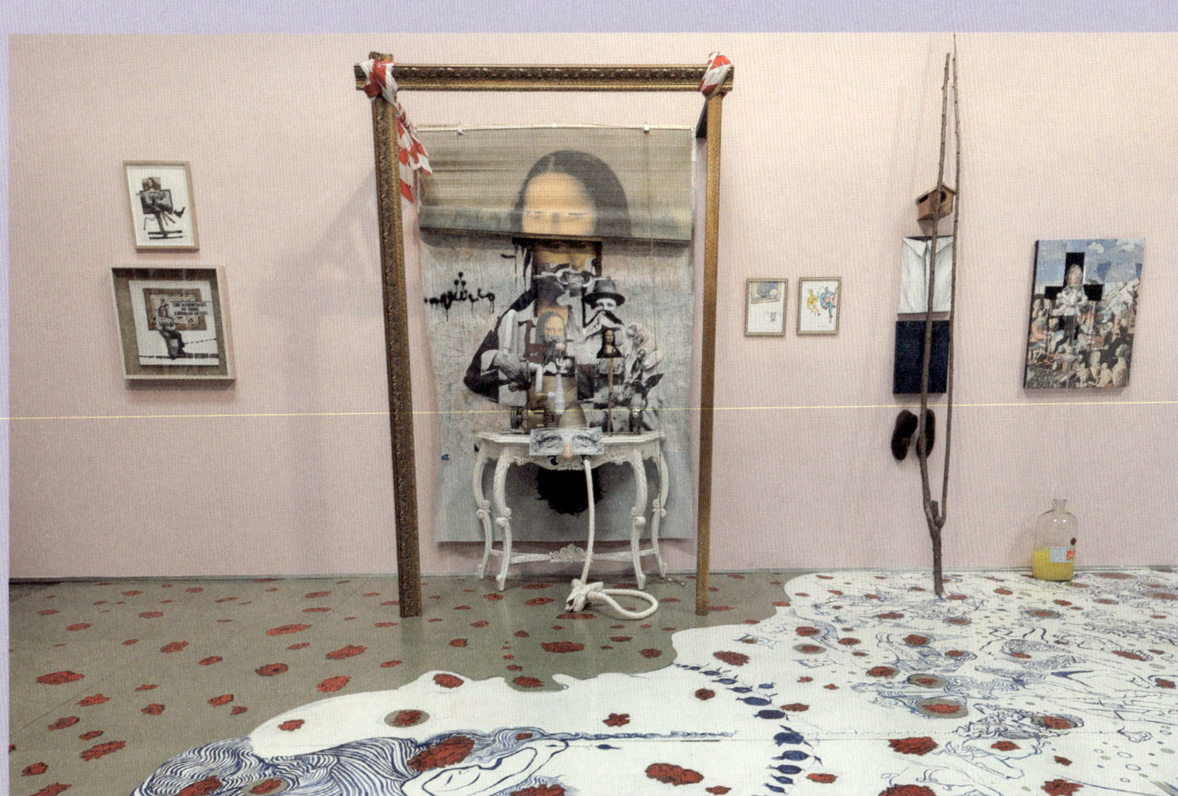

Left to right, Ramin Haerizadeh, *The Emperor's New Dress*, 2013, Collage and ink on paper, 35.5 x 25.5 cm; Ramin Haerizadeh, *The Emperor's New Dress*, 2013, Paper collage, acrylic, ink and pencil on cardboard, 45 x 44 cm; Ramin Haerizadeh, *The Emperor's New Dress*, 2014, Paper collage and spray paint on canvas, ornamented gilded frames sticks, rattan blind, wooden table, synthetic hair, water pump motor, plastic pipes, goat skull, terracotta sculpture, plastic nose, plastic ribbons, fake chicken leg, 250 x 160 x 100 cm; Daniel Johnston, *Good Luck Laurie and Daniel*, 2000, Marker on paper, 27.94 x 21.59 cm; Daniel Johnston, *Oh My GOD*, 2000, Marker on paper, 27.94 x 21.59 cm; Hesam Rahmanian, *A Suit From Head to Toe*, 2013, Shoes, wooden sticks and acrylic on canvas, 30 x 279 x 30 cm; Ramin Haerizadeh, *Sharbat-e Rooh Afza*, 2013, Paper collage, acrylic and plastic respirator on canvas, water and ink in glass bottle, 187 x 60 x 32 cm

Installation view, *The Exquisite Corpse Shall Drink the New Wine*, 2014

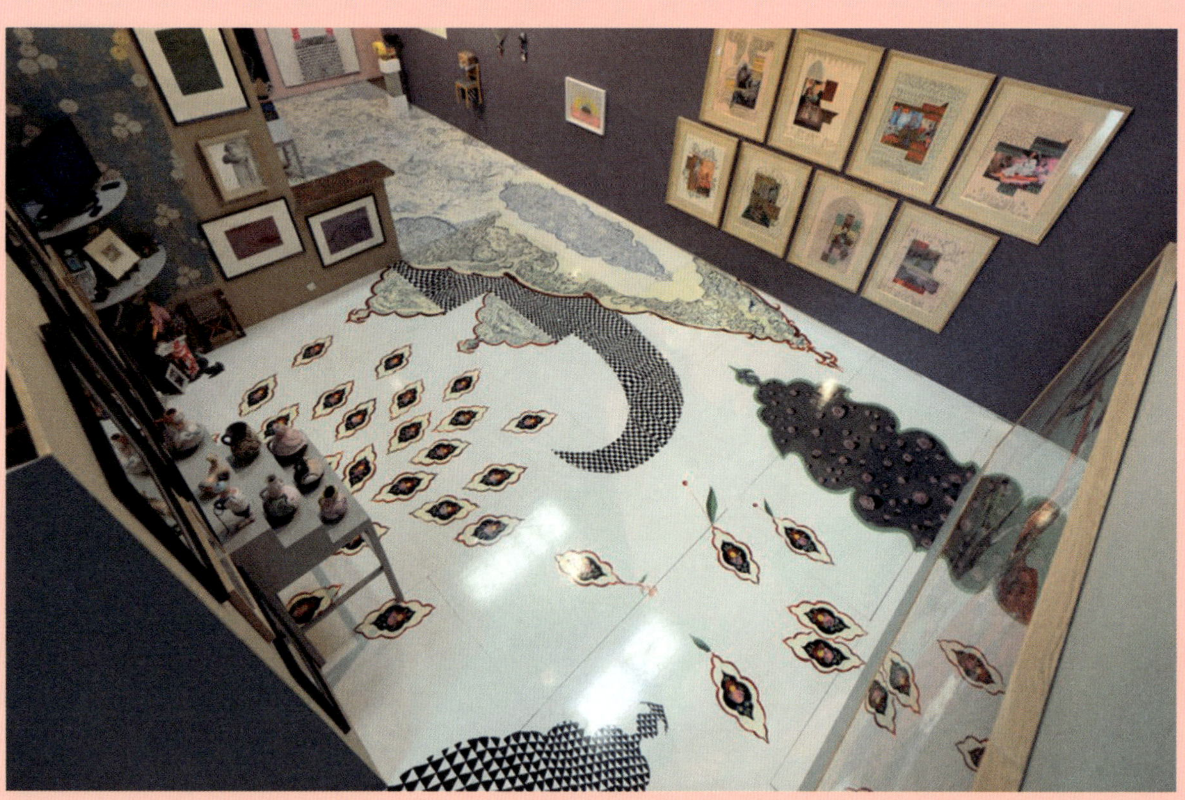

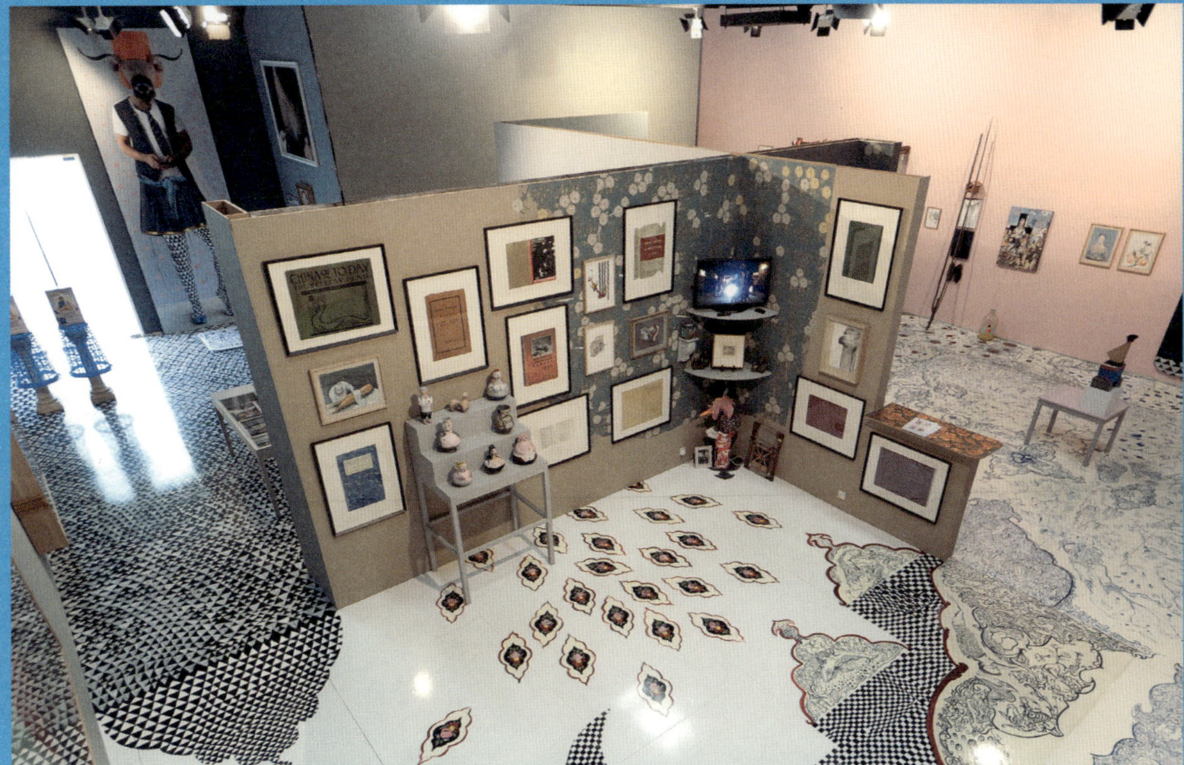

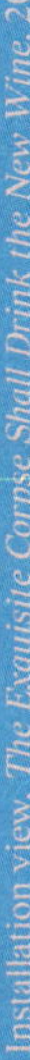

Installation view. *The Exquisite Corpse Shall Drink the New Wine*, 2014

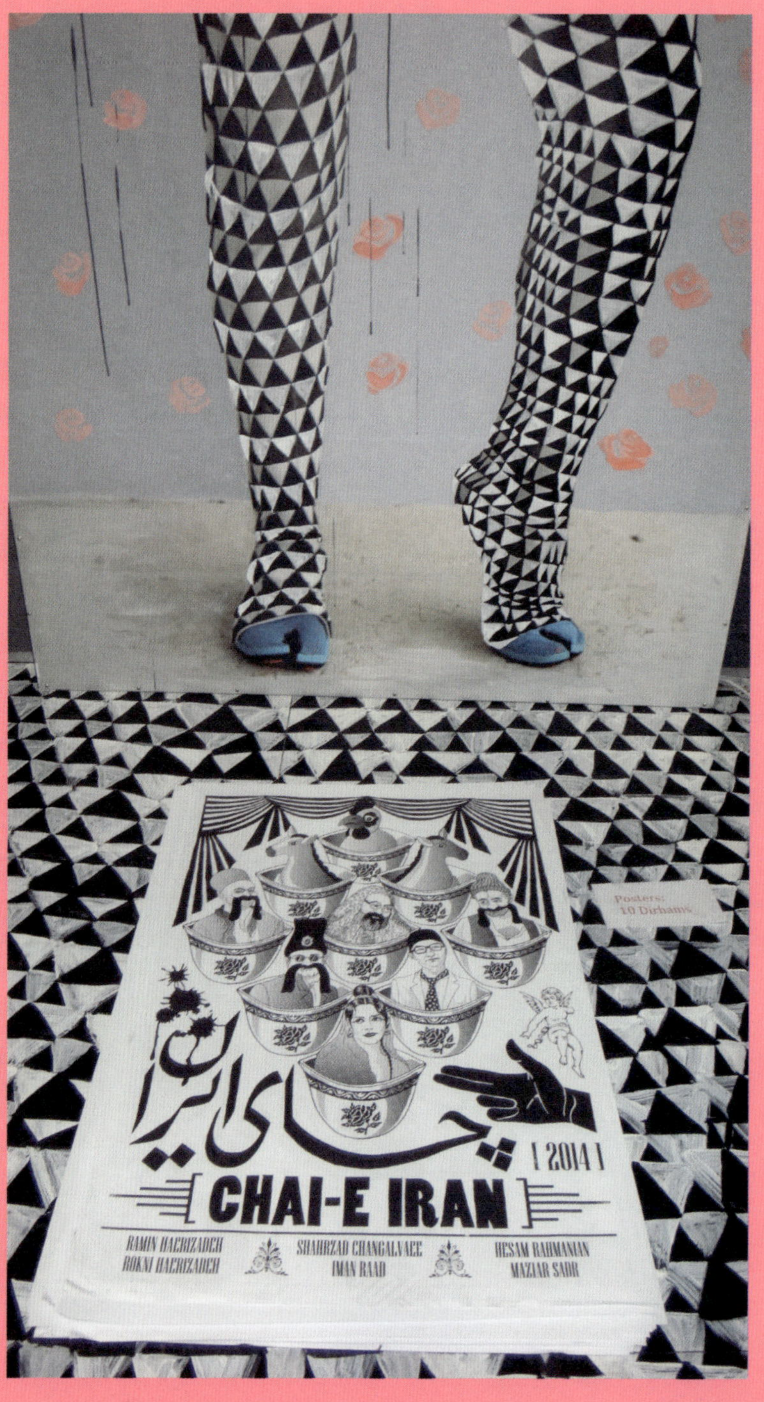
Posters:
10 Dirhams
CHAI-E IRAN
2014
RAMIN HAERIZADEH
ROKNI HAERIZADEH
SHAHRZAD CHANGALVAEE
IMAN RAAD
HESAM RAHMANIAN
MAZIAR SADR

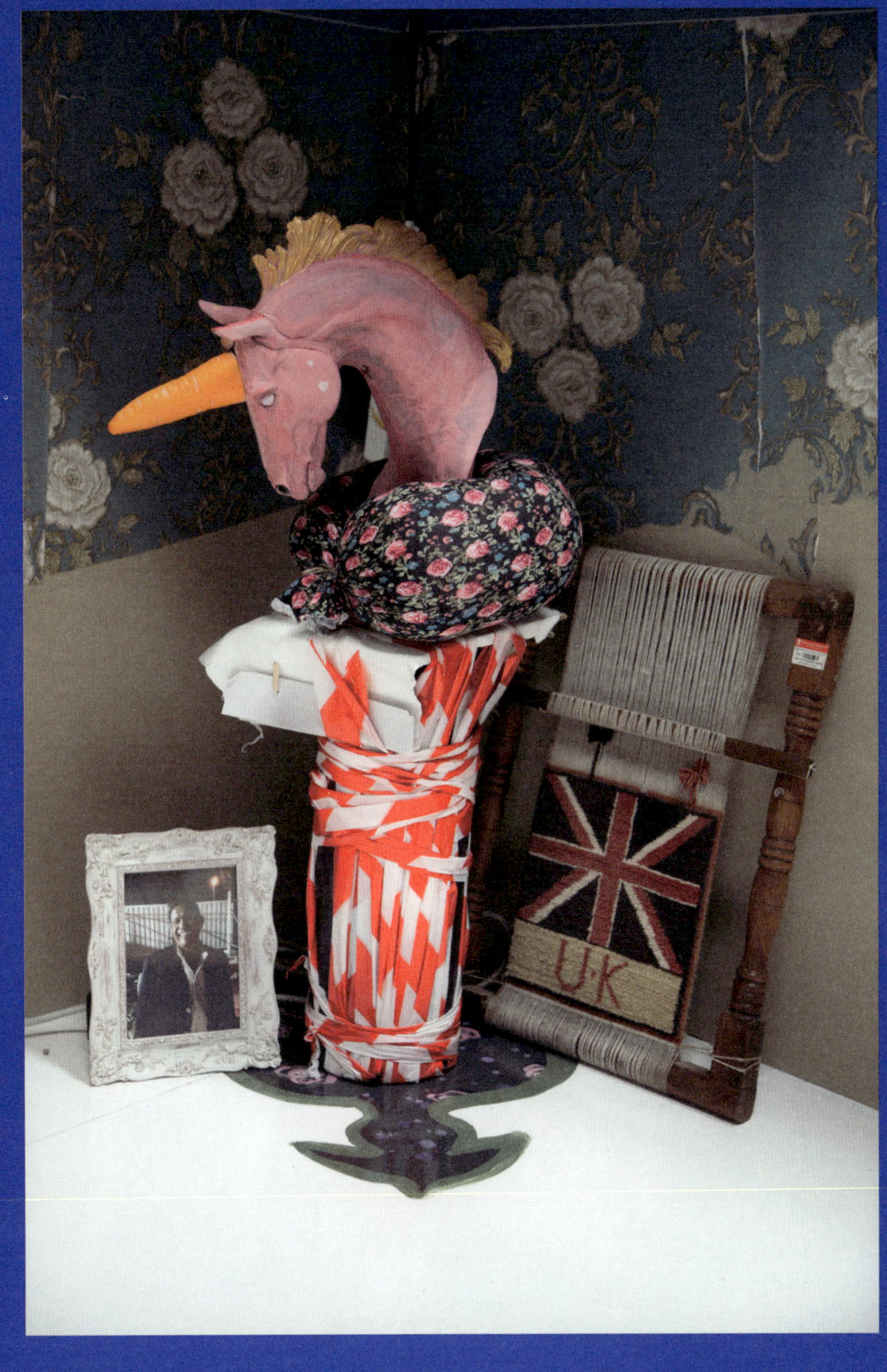

Installation view, *The Exquisite Corpse Shall Drink the New Wine*, 2014,
Including readymades, resin unicorn, acrylic paint, stuffed leggings, cardboard and plastic ribbon
Variable dimensions

INDEX

Page 24

top:

A woman said to her husband, "You of rotting balls!"

To which he answered, "And how could they not, having pilgrimed the path of your flower for forty years?"

bottom:

A soldier was asked, "Why aren't you out fighting the infidels?"

The solider replied, "I swear to God – I don't know them, they don't know me. How could we be enemies?"

Page 25

top:

They asked a Zoroastrian, "How do you interpret the divine Writ, 'The Lord has given, and the Lord has taken?'"

The Zoroastrian replied, "As for an interpretation, I do not know. But I will tell you this: it is not the thing to be said at a reception, nor at a wedding, nor when good company is being enjoyed."

bottom:

A man went to a faqih (expert in Islamic law) and said, "I am a Hanbali, I performed my ablutions and prayed to Ahmad ibn Hanbal's religion. But during my prayer, I felt a dampness in my pants; it was dirty and had a foul smell."

The faqih said, "God bless you. All religions would agree that you have soiled yourself."

Page 26

top:

An Arab was told: "You have grown old and done nothing with your life. Why don't you repent and make the Hajj."

The Arab said, "I do not have enough money to make the pilgrimage."

"So sell your house."

"But where would I live upon my return? And if I don't come back, should I sleep beside the Kaa'ba? Won't God then say, 'Hey, you pathetic loser, why did you sell your house only to come here and live in mine?'"

bottom:

A man whose wife had grown dissatisfied was asked, "Is there anyone that can bring peace between the two of you?" The man replied, "The thing that brought us peace has died."

Page 27

top:

Abu Zayd: "I could no longer find a woman who could sheath my sword, until I chanced upon one. I entered her gradually, then asked: 'May I take my leave?' to which her reply was, 'An insect descended upon a palm tree and said to it, 'Steady yourself, I am going to fly off!'

The palm replied, 'How can I feel you taking off when I did not feel you descend?'"

bottom:

A man requested a hairless teenage boy from the procurers but was brought a slave girl instead. "I do not want her!" the man said.

"Do you want a more beautiful one?"

"No I prefer one with a bulge," he said.

"In that case," said the procurer, "plant a carrot in her shame and affix two onions to it, then take her from the back and consider her afresh."

Page 28

top:

Murawiya was known for his patience. No one could enrage him. Then, a man arrived to court and claimed that he could. The man said: "I ask of you, marry your mother to me for she has a big, hard backside."

"That was the reason my father adored her," replied Murawiya.

bottom:

A man said to a woman, "I want to taste you to find out who is sweeter, you or my wife."

"Ask my husband," said the woman, "for he has tasted me and tasted her."

Page 29

top:

Muzabbid said to his wife, "Do allow me to enwrap you from behind."

She replied: "But my back and front are close friends, I don't want to make one jealous of the other!"

bottom:

While Muzabbid's wife was pregnant, she looked at his face and said, "Woe to me if what is in my belly should look like you."

"Woe to you if it should not!" he replied.

Page 30

top:

A man passed a beautiful woman on the road and stopped to stare at her. So she said, "Do not stare, for your staff will rise but someone else will lead me."

bottom:

A woman said, "Someone had me as if he wanted my centre to yield a treasure from the Jahiliyya age."

Page 31

top:

Upon falling sick, a woman said to her husband, "Woe to you, what will you do should I die?"

"What will I do should you not die?" he replied.

bottom:

A woman went to a judge and complained: "My husband is not fulfilling my rights, and I'm still a young woman. I am not satisfied with less than five times every night."

I am not a braggart, and I am not capable of more than three times," said the man.

"Incredible!" exclaimed the judge. "Every time a claim comes to me, I end up offering something from myself. I'll take responsibility for the remaining two times."

Page 32

top:

Abou El-Eina came to the table and was served a not-so-sweet faloodeh*. He said, "This faloodeh was made before God had spoken to the honey bee."

**A Persian sorbet of thin vermicelli noodles with cold starch and rosewater.*

bottom:

Obadeh was asked, "What did your daughter inherit from her husband?"

He replied, "Four months and ten days."

Page 33

top:

On her wedding night, a woman passed

wind and was so ashamed that she wept. "Do not cry," her husband comforted her, "for the rumble of a bride is a sign of abundance."

"So should I release myself again?"

"No, we don't have the room for any more abundance."

bottom:
A woman called her husband a cuckold and destitute. "Thank God, I'm the innocent one here," said the man, "for you are to blame for the first and God for the second."

VIDEOS
In chronological order

Night Of Another Spring, 2013 – 2014
In 2012, the artists improvised and photographed Jean Genet's 'The Maids' in their living room. This led to a fascination with the love-hate power struggle between Genet's Madame and her servants that addresses how the powerless take on the worst characteristics of their oppressors in an act of mimicry. The similarity between a portrait of Marie Antoinette and a friend of the artists' was the starting point for 'Night Of Another Spring.'

Fragments of 'The Green Automobile' by Allen Ginsberg are heard as Madame is escorted to an exhibition by her butler and a fan-waving servant. She has her photograph taken with the artworks and, after a sacrificial feast, meets her buxom lady-in-waiting who both flatters and teases her. We hear a poem by Forough Farrokhzad while Madame gives birth to a pig. She vigorously washes black paint from her courtier's head, torments her butler with sit-ups and picks a flower to slip in her corset. She is consequently tried by a judge and condemned to death. Later, her courtiers eat pizza, and Madame's severed head is on the table.

Chai-e Iran, 2013 – 2014
The artists found a cheap tea caddy decorated with a painted scene of a veiled tea-picker standing in an idyllic, serene tea field. The video imagines the life of this tea-picker, as seen through the melodramatic, dance-orientated lens of a Film Farsi – a Bollywood-like pop cinema that proliferated before 1979 and is today largely remembered with syrupy nostalgia or dismissed as an immoral relic. Like any true Film Farsi tragedy, the lead in Chai-e Iran moves from humble obscurity to stardom before she meets an inevitable death.

After being woken by a cockerel, and leaving her dear mother for the tea fields, the tea-picker dreams of buying tea from a supermarket. Two horsemen arrive and attempt to woo the tea-picker, occasionally lifting her dress. She meets with her lover, an intellectual, before she is taken to dance for an amorous khan, a wealthy landowner. The tea picker remains faithful to the intellectual, however, and they marry.

The tea-picker listens to her husband reading and her clothes change to that of a political activist. During a protest, she knocks a solider's hat off and wields a traffic cone before her death by shooting is caught on camera in a moment eerily similar to the tragic fate of Neda Agha-Soltan, killed during the 2009 post-election demonstrations in Tehran.

O, You People!, 2014
'O, You People!' records a two-week-long ritual on a stilted boathouse in the Gulf of Mexico. The work began from a poem by Nima Yushij, widely regarded as the initiator of modern poetry in Iran. Yushij's 'O You People' (Ay Adam-ha) describes a man thrashing about in the surf as he drowns, calling out to well-fed bathers relaxing on-shore. In the video, male and female voice-overs are heard reading an 'unfaithful' version of the poem: the original was translated word-by-word from Farsi to English by a bilingual speaker, then put back together as a poem by an English-speaking writer in collaboration with the trio.

Ramin, Rokni and Hesam rose every morning at 4am, and filmed each other moving around the boathouse until sunrise – sniffing the floorboards, offering their nipples to the wooden railings, pointing to an unseen point in the sea. Occasionally the spoken words of the poem mirror the artists' gestures but the solemnity of the text is constantly undercut by the absurdity of the gestures on-screen. The colour the artists wear indicates the day of the week that the performance took place on: Yellow for Sunday, green for Monday, red for Tuesday, blue for Wednesday, brown for Thursday, white for Friday and black for Saturday.

We Are the Eighth of a Kind, 2014 and SPAM, 2014
These two performances took place during the Robert Rauschenberg Foundation's residency programme on Captiva Island, Florida. 'We Are The Eighth of a Kind' is a collaboration with musician and artist Lonnie Holley. Holley plays piano and sings improvised lyrics in response to the performance around him: A donkey hops around the stage on a crutch and a crow in a rubber ring bangs an invisible drum.

'SPAM' is an improvised collaboration with the Native American writer William S. Yellow Coat Jr, who reads one of his signature 'Spam Rants'. The text describes a vision at a Bruce Springsteen concert, in which the narrator imagines being processed into Spam and searching in the dark for a mysterious 'Clint'. In the background, a butcher sharpens his knives and rips apart red and yellow rubbery objects.

Foolad, 2014 – 2015

'Foolad' means steel in Farsi. The work begins like a hard-boiled anti-hero movie: a woman in a catsuit walks through the streets at dawn, holding two pistols. After entering the artists' home, she 'fights' a series of banal stock characters and stereotypes who are defeated by being transformed into domestic products like a blender and a vacuum cleaner. One of the defeated combatants puts on an afro wig, initiating an impromptu rave. Afterwards, the cat-suited woman lies sleeping, as her former opponents stand around her body plotting to rape her.

The soundtrack includes excerpts of the video game Tekken, early animations by Noureddin Zarrinkelk, an improvised composition by Nesa Azadikhah, John Cage's 'The Choral Works (I)' and 'Pianos and Voices' by John Cage and Meredith Monk.

Aakkaandi, 2014 – 2015

A pig-faced tourist-curator clutching a tote bag visits a tailoring shop to get a new dress copied. A doctor, and his violently shushing nurse, administers everything from injections to dental reconstruction. Shots of a stunned bird reawakening are accompanied by a Gurulu mask dance. Improvised with Idrani Sirisena and Edward St, who live and work at the villa that the artists share, these short, simple vignettes are interspersed with the couple's recollections of the Sri Lankan Civil War and the political machinations that stoked the conflict. The work culminates in a collaboratively painted canvas that they steadily layer with Tamil lettering. Several sections of 'Aakkaandi' were filmed by Edward St. Many of the images in this video are inspired by the works of Tamil poets, particularly 'The Aakkaandi Bird' by Shanmugam Sivalingam and '21 May 1986' by R. Cheran.

FLOATING SCULPTURES

Page 23, 34, 36, 40, 64, 67, 92, 97
Rokni Haerizadeh,
Tourists, 2013
Acrylic paint on terracotta,
Group of eight
25 x 15 x 21 cm

Page 99
Ramin Haerizadeh,
Cabinet of Self-Curiosities, 2012
Fibreglass, clay and ink sculpture,
wooden picture frames, photographs,
soft toys and stones
177 x 80 x 43 cm

Acknowledgments

We are grateful to the following people in helping
this book come together:

Abdelmonem Bin Eisa Alserkal
Fiza Akram
Joan Ayunan
Daniel Baumann
Hengameh Basseghi
Edoardo Bonaspetti
Stefano Cernuschi
Jean-Marc Decrop
Olivier Delfosse
Annabel Holt
Mohammed Jabri
Vilma Jurkute
Miskid Lau
The Robert Rauschenberg Foundation
Maaziar Sadr
Arnaud van den Eynde

The artists, editors and Kunsthalle Zürich would like to
thank Gallery Isabelle van den Eynde and Alserkal Avenue
who made the production of this book possible.

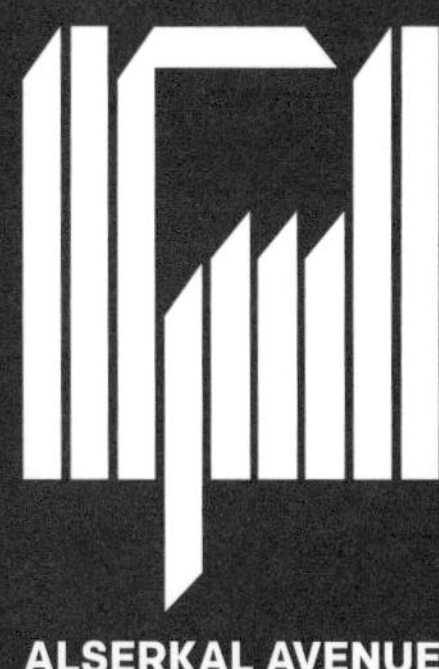

ALSERKAL AVENUE

Colophon

Published on the occasion of *Slice A Slanted Arc Into Dry Paper Sky*
Ramin Haerizadeh, Rokni Haerizadeh, Hesam Rahmanian
Kunsthalle Zürich, Switzerland, February 21 – May 17, 2015

Edited by Tina Kukielski
Co-edited by Christopher Lord
Texts by Tina Kukielski, Daniel Baumann and Christopher Lord
Translation by Nazli Ghassemi

Design by Ghazaal Vojdani

Photography by Musthafa Aboobacker (seeing things), Xavier Ansart, Scott Barfield, Ramin Haerizadeh, Rebecca Rees, and Maaziar Sadr
Page IV: *Ta'ziyeh* images courtesy Mehr News Agency
Pages III – XV include installation shots from *I Put It There You Name It* (2012) and *The Exquisite Corpse Shall Drink the New Wine* (2014) showing the incorporation of other artists' work.
All installation views, pages 89 – 103, Gallery Isabelle van den Eynde, Dubai

Mousse Publishing
Via De Amicis 53 - 20123 Milano
moussepublishing.com

Ramin Haerizadeh, Rokni Haerizadeh and Hesam Rahmanian
ISBN 9788867491353

© Ramin Haerizadeh, Rokni Haerizadeh, Hesam Rahmanian, the authors, Gallery Isabelle van den Eynde, Mousse Publishing

Printed in Italy